Reclaim your throne.
Own your crown.
Embrace the Tigress within.
The world is waiting.

UNSTOPPABLE TENACITY

Erica Stepteau

Copyright © 2017 by Erica Stepteau

All rights reserved, including the right of reproduction in whole or part in any format.

First edition published February, 2017.
All production design are trademarks of Erica Stepteau, used under license.

For information regarding bulk purchases of this book, digital purchase and special discounts, please contact the publisher.

Manufactured in the United States of America

Title ID: 6875420
ISBN-13: 978-1542655422

PRAISE FOR UNSTOPPABLE TENACITY

"Erica Stepteau has written a grounded and thorough examination of what it is to charge forth with unstoppably tenacity. Through real life examples, sass, charm, and intelligence, she navigates this difficult topic in a way that is not only practical, but inspiring. This is a great read for anyone who wants to see radical shifts in their life from the inside out and who are ready to reclaim their throne and the tigress within."
- **Rocky Callen, Bestselling Novelist and Entrepreneur**

"Erica is one of those Phenomenal Women that Maya Angelou talked about! Her testimony alone could change somebody's life!"
-Marguerite Chandler

"Tenacity at its Finest! So, inspiring!"
-Mia Trevillion

"Wow! Wow! Wow! Erica Stepteau! Yes, girl SLAYYYYYY! This was so amazing to read. Just shows how strong you really are!!" **-Anji C.**

"Erica is the QUEEN of creativity and visibility!! Optimum creativity and strategy can happen in an hour! Erica is the master at getting clear and creative and always showing up, probably the biggest lessons I have learned from her. If you feel stuck getting visible girls, Erica is your girl!! Thank you for all that you have done to help me!"
-Melissa Ramirez

"Your story has given me hope and renewed my courage."
-Liliana Sampica

"Erica is the epitome of what it means to believe in yourself and to dare greatly!"
-Melinda Williamson

"Erica is amazing and even with one simple conversation with her, I feel like wonder woman!"
-Inez Ruiz

"Erica is a real gem. Working with her has been a true blessing as she is a very powerful, genuine and inspiring coach. She knows what questions to ask to make you move forward step by step. She gives a lot of helpful input and pushes you with clarity and passion, in a refreshingly positive way towards your goals. It's an honor to work with her and I highly recommend her services!" **-Bea Jucker:**

"I love love love the energy Erica brings. It jumps out from the pages in all the best ways. She continues to show up for herself and for others." **-Jaime Drummond:**

To My Dear Mother

A woman who has been burned many times, but chose to blaze.

"She survived because the fire inside her burned brighter than the fire around her."

- Joshua Graham

PREFACE
(What's all this Tenacity Talk?)

> "Tenacity doesn't mean you 'work hard'; it means you continually improve yourself from the inside out and enjoy the journey as you persistently strive towards your goals."
> - Erica Stepteau

Is this you? You are ready for a change in your life and ready to put action in, but just don't know where to start. You struggle with consistency in many departments in your life including business, health, and personal goals. You find yourself jumping from one thought to another feeling empty and purposeless. Yet, you hear a small whisper saying, "there is more".

I am here to declare: You are a Queen. You might not know it yet; you might feel alone or small or not enough. But I am here to tell you that it is time to shake out your hair and grab your crown. Your power is based in the tenacity of your heart -- because only with unflinching faith and relentless action, can you claim your throne.

A true queen has grace, poise, confidence, intelligence and a warrior spirit because no matter what, she will stand for her kingdom, her legacy, her truth and no one will deny it of her.

It's time to be the tenacious woman God called you to be. Most of the time it's our emotional baggage and gremlins preventing us from being "unstoppable". My sole purpose is to empower women to be tenacious on their journey by pushing beyond thoughts of scarcity, past failures, potential obstacles, or lack of resources. In this book, you will obtain step-by-step actions on how to expand yourself until your rubber band of limitations snaps, turn challenges into opportunities, and examine the conditions of your heart in order to rise up and claim your UNSTOPPABLE TENACITY!

Tenacity is a learned trait. It takes a lot of self-love, consistency, and determination to make it happen and you, my friend, CAN make your dreams happen.

> **"My life today is a result of constantly stretching the muscles that built my character. I recognize now that the most uncomfortable moments were those when I was pushed beyond my perceived limits. Those were usually the times that I thought I was already playing big but was asked to play bigger. Are you being asked to play bigger?" – Lisa Nichols**

Lisa Nichols inspired this book. I was sitting in my office, listening in on a private group call with this powerhouse woman and she said something that hit me. She told us how our power rested in our story – as painful or difficult as it might be – and that it was our story that needed to be honored and shared. It all hit me at that moment: all my pain, heartaches, confusion, and losses were all aligned and purposeful for me to share with women to empower them to rise up and claim their unstoppable power towards the life they dream to achieve.

I am relentless in this vision, because I have seen the power in a woman who is brimming over with tenacity and intention.

Unstoppable Tenacity

=

Infinite Blessings.

All you have to do is claim your inheritance!

The movement is rumbling, growing, igniting.

Be brave and join it.

TENACIOUS QUEENS UNITE!

CONTENTS

PRAISE FOR UNSTOPPABLE TENACITY.....................3

PREFACE..6

Claim your Inheritance..14

Your Net Worth...17

The Power to Know thy Self...20

Vulnerability to Heal and Transform............................30

Shame doesn't have to be Part of your Story................34

Shifting into Royalty Language.....................................40

Slay Limiting Thoughts...42

Silencing the Gremlins..46

Release Resistance..49

Journey to Self-Love...57

Drop F.E.A.R – (False Evidence Appearing Real)......62

Tapping into your Inner Child.......................................67

You Can Have It All...76

The Power of Visualization...82

Break the Complacency Curse......................................90

Setting Yourself up For Success....................................95

Fresh Start...99

Snap your Rubber band Snap......................................103

Rewrite your Story..105

Setting Goals (Long & Short-term)................................. ...108

It's Time to Slay... 115

Take Control of your Life.. 121

The Power of Tenacity... ...128

Find the Champion Within....................................... 135

Importance of your Environment................................. 143

Earth Angel to the Rescue....................................... 148

Fail Forward.. 155

Purify your Heart: Let Go of Bitterness........................ 160

What's your Money Story?....................................... 167

Mastering your Feminine Energy................................. ...175

Manage Your Sexual Energy......................................179

It's ok to Shrink..184

Be an Unstoppable Queen..188

Queen Rituals (Consistency is Key)..............................191

Managing Change..196

Dealing with Uncertainty..205

Manage your Energy...211

Shutdown the Comparison..214

Ruffle the Feathers & Speak your Truth...........................220

Embrace the Path..223

CONCLUSION..230

BONUS TOOLS..232

ACKNOWLEGEMENTS……………………………….233

ABOUT THE AUTHOR……………………………..235

NOTES & RECOMMENDED READINGS…………237

SECTION 1:
MAKE SPACE FOR THE VISION

Chapter 1
Claim your Inheritance

> "When you see yourself as the Queen that you are, you shine and those high vibrations attract success like a magnet." - Erica Stepteau

There was a time in my life when it was hard to get out of bed in the morning. I was lost in overwhelm, feeling defeated, and felt beaten down by depression. It was right after my third miscarriage and I found myself throwing fits, tossing things, drinking during the day, just to mask my emotions which left me feeling completely helpless and alone. Every day was a battle; I was lost in a fog and no longer living. I was in survival mode and not even able to recognize who I was in the mirror.

But then something changed. I was reminded that I had greatness within me. I had forgotten that truth somewhere along the way, but in a moment, I remembered. And in that moment, I decided I needed to change my life so that I could claim the crown that was destined for me.

As I was emerging from my brokenness and owning my power, I was scrolling online and came across Baylor Barbee's chess approach to life & business, what he said woke me up and paved the way to the rest of my journey.

"Every day you define your role; how you move, how you operate, how you plan. In chess, a pawn can move one space, at most two spaces. A Queen on the other hand can

*move in **ANY Direction**, as far as she wants. Think about your life. There are no limitations on how much you can accomplish in a day. No one will ever tell you, you've gone too far today, you've accomplished too much, and you must stop here. We place those limitations on ourselves sometimes. We don't strive for royalty; we settle for being pawns.*

God doesn't want that for us. God wants us to move about freely, He wants us to cover "the entire board." That's why He put us on it. In Chess, inexperienced players usually sacrifice their pawns early in the game and try and protect "the important pieces." Losing a pawn doesn't affect us, but losing a Bishop, a Queen, and especially a King hurts us. In life, we define our roles based on the decisions we make. Too many people lead careless, uncalculated lives, running right into devastation.

Look at people you admire and look up to. There's a good chance they live their lives as royalty. They put a solid support group around them. They work well with others. They make calculated moves and they plan very well. Aside from that, when it's time to make a move in life, they strike hard and cover a lot of ground. You can do the same. You CAN be a Queen on this Chess Board of Life. All it takes is a change in your mindset. You must live your life as a piece that matters, and subsequently, people around you will start treating you as such."

Inspired by this quote and the principle of living as a queen, I radically overhauled my life and am devoted to helping and inspiring other women to do the same. I am here to remind you, whoever you are and wherever you are, that you have infinite power within you, even if you don't feel it right now. And that power is what you need to tap into in order to claim your inheritance.

I am here to hold your hand and push you every step of the way back to your throne.

Every chapter, I will challenge you to "slay". This is key to becoming the Queen you truly are, so don't just close the book after each chapter, take time to get quiet and reflect and then act.

Here is your initiation into that process. Get ready. It's time to slay.

 *Time to Slay:*

Write down the following questions and reflect on your answers in your Unstoppable Tenacity journal:

- How can you claim your inheritance today and step into your power?
- What's holding you back from your true potential?
- What will you have to give up in to make room for your dream?
- In what ways, have you been playing like a pawn?
- What makes it hard for you to see yourself as value in your own eyes or acknowledge your purpose to serve your kingdom (the world)?
- What does the Queen in you desire?

Chapter 2
Your Net Worth

> **"When your self-worth goes up, your net worth goes up with it."- Mark Victor Hansen**

I wouldn't be shocked if after the first chapter that you may feel triggered by the fact of thinking of yourself as a "Queen". You're probably thinking to yourself, "I don't look like a Queen" or "I don't have the same resources/money as someone considered royalty". Well, I am calling you out today! God has called you to be a Queen who impacts the world with her gifts in a major way.

You are worthy to be a queen no matter the amount in your bank account, past mistakes, or even if you are confused on your path. You don't have to have it all together. I want you to examine the traits of a Queen as inspiration and as confirmation to your birthright without being critical of yourself.

To become a queen, you must think as a queen. In order to think like a Queen, you must know what she represents:

- She is confident, poised, and knows her worth.

- A queen also has a greater purpose than just herself. She uses her authority for a worthwhile cause, and she does so wisely.

- She conducts herself with self-respect, authority, and class, self-possessed woman

> whom others can rely on. She is a confidant and a source of wisdom – she can take care of herself and others.
>
> - That being said, she also does not *overthink* to the point where it impedes action. She is a decision-maker and a leader.

A woman carries herself in a different way when she knows her worth. You will no longer accept the life you were complacent with before nor hang around the same people you were with before. There should be a burning desire to want more now that you are aware of your higher net worth.

Throughout this book, I will be referring to you as a Queen or even a Tenacious Queen at times. Each chapter will help you remove layers so that you are able to move freely on your path. Tenacity is an ongoing learned trait which you embrace throughout this book. I want to officially welcome you to Queendomville! Your life will never be the same!

Let's get Tenacious Queens.

 Time to Slay:

- In what ways, can you increase your self-worth? What normally boosts your confidence and make you feel good about yourself?

- How can you add value to the experiences you have encountered or embrace the Queen "persona"?

- How can you respect yourself more and give yourself credit for accomplishments and your journey?

- What symbols or reminders do you need to ensure you are reminded on a daily basis of increased net worth?

Chapter 3
The Power to Know thy Self

> **"Make it your business to know thyself, which is the most difficult lesson in the world. Yet from this lesson thou will learn to avoid the frog's foolish ambition of swelling to rival the bigness of the ox."**
> –Miguel de Cervantes

For over two decades, I walked around aimlessly serving and moving along the journey with little understanding of who I was supposed to emulate or what capacity I should be serving in. Now I see that the biggest struggle for me was not knowing myself. It took me a very long time to see that I was walking around masking the true Erica to numb my pain. I remember in school trying to make everyone happy and be like everyone. I didn't hang out with a specific group of people because I truly didn't know who I was and what I stood for. I had no identity, but I used my "gift for gab" to catch others' attention. It wasn't always positive reactions, but I got their attention.

The biggest resistance I had was to let people see the real me. The real Erica couldn't trust anyone because of the sexual abuse I experienced as a child and lack of self-love which resulted in having a "chip" on my shoulder. I was hurt, bitter, and just down-right confused. I was angry and had a whole lot of attitude. I remember a conversation I had with the First Lady of a church I attended in 2004 like it was yesterday, she shared with me that I wasn't being the "Real Erica". I instantly became offended thinking, "who is she to tell me that I am being fake"? It took me well over 10 years to reflect on that conversation and agree with her. When I came to the realization that I didn't truly know myself, I began to immerse my energy into personal development and self-evaluation. I wanted to know myself inside and out. I didn't want to leave any stone unturned so I took many tests including Myer Briggs, Strengths based Leadership, and Keirsy Temperament personality profiles as well as deep dived into my desires and the pain that I had avoided for so long.

If you do not know yourself, it becomes easier to copy others which forces you not to be authentic and prevents your expansions to be the most optimum self. Also, not knowing yourself forces you to constantly seek validation from others. When people compliment you, it should be confirmations of things you already know about yourself! Use your strength and weaknesses to gain leverage on how to approach your goals.

For me, my strengths are determination and optimism. I know how to get people pumped/motivated. I am an action taker and very good at helping people get unstuck to move forward.

My weaknesses at times can be my ambition; I must constantly find balance between action and taking a break. Also, I tend to overlook my progress/success because I am looking so far in the future. To keep the leverage, I have mini milestones to celebrate with FUN things to do (get dressed up/dance/pamper time) for myself since that's important to me and every evening I tell myself what I am proud of achieving or accomplishing. It helps me slow down mentally and acknowledge the work I've done so far and be proud of it.

Mini-milestones allows me to lean into my successes and when we allow ourselves to pause and reflect on how far we have come, it fuels our ability to breed more success.

 Time to Slay:

- Here is a quiz I would like for you try: http://richardstep.com/richardstep-strengthsweaknesses-aptitude-test/free-aptitude-test-findyour-strengthsweaknesses-online-version/

- Share your results in our group page Tenacious Queens Unite on Facebook with the following hashtags: #unstoppabletenacity #timetoslay

- How will you learn more about yourself? What area in your life can benefit from this awareness?

- How can you embrace your imperfections to discover your true source of strength and purpose?

- How can you acknowledge and own your gifts to share with the world?

Chapter 4
Permission to Feel

> "What would happen if you stopped fighting and gave yourself permission to feel? Not just the good things, but everything?"
> – R.J. Anderson

In 2013 my husband (Joshua) and I decided to give In Vitro Fertilization (IVF) a try in hopes of achieving the dream of becoming parents. For those who don't know much about IVF; it is the process of fertilization by manually combining an egg and sperm in a laboratory dish, and then transferring the embryo to the uterus. It is a very long strenuous 6-8-week process of daily needles, vaginal ultrasounds, and raging hormones.

Five percent of couples with fertility issues seek out IVF. With top chances of IVF success have per-cycle success rates of 40% or higher. During a regular cycle, there is a 15-20% chance to conceive naturally in any month for any couple. Our Fertility specialist shared with us before proceeding with IVF and after our 2nd miscarriage that we had a 2% chance of getting pregnant on our own. Hearing such a small number as a chance to become parents was devastating for us. We honestly thought going with IVF would be the answer to solve our uncertainty, frustrations, and void in our hearts.

I remember us being so excited to get started with this because we had just celebrated our 10 year Anniversary/Renewal of Vows ceremony and just knew this was our year! We had thoughts that since we originally married in a courthouse, that maybe we didn't consecrate our marriage effectively in 2003 and God was waiting on us to do it the "right" way before blessing us with a child. When you have tried to achieve a dream for this long, you start creating all types of thoughts and philosophies to the mix to provide deeper understanding to be at peace. As humans, we tend to have to KNOW it all and know WHY something is happening to actually embrace it. Can you relate?

For the first time in our whole marriage we shared with everyone that we were trying to conceive. Before starting the process, we got our friends involved and co-workers. For years, we kept it to ourselves and mourned with BFNs (Big Fat Negative Pregnancy tests) in secret. So, this time around we thought if we shared with others this will automatically manifest the babies we desperately desired. We thought it would rally up prayers, high vibes, and good goo-goo to provide a chance for others to witness a miracle unfold with their human eye.

We just knew it was going to happen this time around, we felt it in our deep core and was so assured God will not let us down since we were being so transparent and open. Everyone was so beyond excited for us and cheering for success. Every day we would have conversations with others about us having twins and how life would be so different and even MORE meaningful.

I began to pin every picture on Pinterest of women pregnant with twins. We even started to pick out nursery colors and themes because we were obsessed with the idea of becoming parents. All of the pics are still on my iPad to this day and when I accidently come across them I feel all the joy and excitement I had at that time to obtain a dream I have been waiting on for over a decade.

As we begin the process, our IVF team assured us we were on track and everything was looking great. No one could tell us there was 100% chance of success, but after doing our baseline biomarkers: hormone levels, ovaries and sperm analysis they felt confident we would be parents as well. Our physician even stated the results we had so far was practically "text book" and this provided to the team even more assurance that this will work for us.

At this time, I was very active and working out with a cool team during lunch hour at a medical device company in Highland Heights, OH. I decided to stop all running which hubby and I did almost every evening in the Metro Parks and the intense Shaun T (Insanity) workout. Instead, I started meditative Yoga. I was really thinking that my high intense physical activity could prevent pregnancy and the success of the IVF process. I didn't want to take a chance since this procedure was close to $25,000 plus the cost of all the injectable medications.

After using contraceptives for approximately 2 weeks to suppress ovarian production we begin the 4-week process of IVF with the crazy daily fertility injections. I remember being so freaked out by putting a needle in my belly. Joshua had to help a lot with this because I would freeze up and start shaking. Around day 5 I started to feel a bit moody and irritated, and the following week I was having all types of meltdowns about food, work, and the feeling of overwhelm. I had to take a leave of absence from work to finish off the IVF process because how crazy I was feeling.

I remember going into the doctor office starting day 5 of cycle every day for blood work and pelvic ultrasounds.

They poked me so much that I began to have bruises on both forearms and I was afraid that I looked like a drug addict. I had to wear long sleeve shirts (thankfully it was still a bit chilly in Ohio) to hid the bruises. And those internal pelvic ultrasounds were so annoying, but I know they had to constantly check how the ovaries were doing during the process. For 7 days, I almost got use to walking in the office getting poked with a needle 2-3 times then jumping on the table and spread my legs open for internal ultrasound.

As we begin to get closer to egg retrieval day the technician stated that one of my ovaries were the size of a golf ball. I already looked 5months pregnant and was beginning to have cramping and very uncomfortable pelvic pain. I believe at this time we had 15-18 follicles (eggs) to use to proceed with process.

Egg retrieval day came. We prayed so hard the night of, we ask God to have his way. At this point of the process I was so bruised and beat up, sore, tired, aggravated, and uncertain on the next steps. As they prepped me for surgery Joshua held my hand and we locked eyes. We didn't say much because we both were very nervous and scared. They grabbed my husband and had him exit room so that they can collect sperm to seal the deal after retrieving my eggs.

I was placed under powerful anesthesia and a needle was passed through the top of my vagina under ultrasound guidance to get to the ovary and follicles. The fluid in the follicles was aspirated through the needed and the eggs detach from the follicle wall and were sucked out of the ovary.

When they completed the 30min surgery, they were able to create 8 embryos. Those were our 8 babies in production.

Now the waiting game starts to see which 2 embryos do they transfer to my uterus. This waiting game can be up to 5 days. We went home and I was still in excruciating pain. I went from pain at a level of 6 on the scale of 1-10 to like a 20 in a matter of one hour. Joshua rushed me to emergency. We explained to them that I just had an egg retrieval surgery. They did an external ultrasound and found that my right ovary ruptured. So yeah, the pain at the rate of 20 made complete sense at that time. I was in so much pain all I did was sleep, they gave me some low dose meds since I was anticipating to put my "babies" in the oven within a few days. We went home the next morning and I was feeling much better.

When we returned home, we were glued to the phone awaiting information about our "babies". The nurse called the first thing that morning and said 3 of them started to dissipate and were not valuable to place in uterus. We started to get sad, but had a very small amount of hope for the other 5. The next day the nurse called again and said 2 more dissolved and then the next day after that she explain we had no more. Our IVF failed. We were crushed because we told everybody and their mama that we will be parents this time. We thought the vulnerability would be the key and sharing our story will solidify our dream. I questioned God on this decision and outcome.

We were very lost on how to move forward at this time. I took another week off work on FMLA because I was so depressed and humiliated. I was disappointed in myself thinking maybe I ate something wrong, didn't relax enough, or missed a step with injections. I also felt horrible that my hubby had to endure all the mood swings, nagging, and errands to accommodate me along the journey without providing to him a very special gift of a child. I was worried about how hubby felt.

He was so sad and there was a lot of silence for a few days in the house. He went to work and came home, I cooked, we ate and that was it. Neither one of us wanted to talk about it. Our phones were blowing up. Everyone wanted to send their condolences, we received flowers in the mail, encouraging text messages, and when I returned to work my team even had a card for me.

After a few days, I allowed myself to actually feel the pain and allowed a few to witness the pain and know that I was struggling to keep my faith and sanity.

What I learned from this particular situation is that it's important to give yourself permission to feel. Since this incident, I have been able to share my journey to fertility a bit more with ease and flow. Sharing has allowed me to heal some deep wounds associated with this journey. Not that every layer is healed, but I am better off allowing myself to feel the pain instead of hoarding it and allowing it to kill me internally.

It's something liberating about allowing yourself to feel, don't numb emotions or play like everything is ok. It's ok to be vulnerable. Find a confidant who is willing to be present NOT just provide guidance or their input. Remember you can't specifically numb these feelings without numbing joy in your life at the same time. So, cry, yell, scream, and grieve when you have to then get back up with confidence and assurance that it will be ok.

 *Time to Slay:*

- Journal thoughts about a time you needed to "feel" instead of masking emotions. As you reflect back, allow yourself to scream, yell, cry, or grieve when necessary.

- How have you lost your tolerance of vulnerability? You cannot selectively numb sections of vulnerability because by default you will numb your joy. The best ways to embrace vulnerability is to have gratitude for all your blessings and give yourself permission to feel.

- What masks are you wearing? In what ways, will you start removing them? What is your biggest fear of exposing yourself?

Chapter 5
Vulnerability to Heal and Transform

> "Vulnerability sounds like truth and like courage. Truth and courage aren't always comfortable, but they are never weakness."
> –Brene Brown

As a child, I was emotionally stifled and forced to push feelings aside. Whether it was to share how I felt physically or emotionally, there was no space to do so. When I would say, I was sick, I was told to go sit down. When I wanted to share how I felt about a particular topic, I was told to be quiet. I never felt like I could be ME and express my deeper thoughts. I honestly don't remember having any heart-to-heart conversations at home as a child. I was actually made fun of because I would constantly watch the Wizard of Oz and cry like a baby. Somehow my deep intuition knew I needed space for healing and an outlet to expose my emotions. However, the reaction to my behavior led me to believe that crying or any feeling of emotions was a sign of weakness.

The problem was I was deeply hurt, but no one wanted to speak about it. At the age of 6 years old My mom was still heavily into crack cocaine, she dropped me off at an unfamiliar apartment; I woke up looking for her, but instead I was awakened by a man foundling me in my private area. I remember it like it was yesterday, the man telling me to be quiet and stop crying. I remember that uncomfortable feeling of being out of control. I was seeking help and no one to be found. I couldn't believe what was going on and became very scared and started trembling with tears coming down my face. I blacked out and woke up on my stomach with semen on my butt. I honestly can't remember if he penetrated me or not. All I know is that I was SCARED, I cried, but no one heard me. I went to sleep and my father found me somehow in this apartment. He grabbed me and took me home back to my mom. At the age of approximately 6 years old I told myself to NEVER trust a man again in my life.

That moment onward I had a serious chip on my shoulder which took many years to remove. I was too young to understand, however that is when the masks started to appear in my life. Soon after this event I found myself living with my aunt. I believe family members heard of this incident and immediately stepped in to force my mom to change her habits. As I discussed in previous chapter, my mom DID change her life. My mom was in rehab for 1year while I stayed with my aunt, uncle, and their kids. I remember her calling me and telling me she will see me soon and things will be better when she returns.

When I reflect back on those calls, I remember hearing the guilt and tremble in my mom's voice. She was so beyond sorry for the environment and suffering she placed me in. She just didn't know how to voice it to me. Her lack of vulnerability began to create a wedge in our relationship and resentment began to rise in my heart towards her. With the help of God, I had to heal myself through all the traumatic experiences, forgive mom, and shed the many layers of masks. It wasn't until I was in my 30s that I became aware of what I was doing. Since I was emotionally stifled as a child and wasn't able to freely share my thoughts and emotions, I became what people thought I should be.

I would copy others or do stuff just to make others happy (which made me a great sales person). With all the years of masking and people pleasing I lost my own identity. Whew! Erica was extremely hard to find; it's been a whirlwind of locating this girl. I had to give myself permission to cry many nights, forgive myself for all the crap I've allowed to cover my true identity, and invest in a lot of books and resources. I shed many layers to get to the core of Erica. I am still a work in progress. However, I feel so much more free in being ME: The ambitious, sassy, playful, and intuitive chic who loves empowering women to see their purpose and value.

I really felt like God has been guiding me all along to be where I am today. Every hurt, roller coaster ride, confusion, and dip in my life has brought me to such a wonderful place. I could be very resentful and bitter about a lot of things (which you will learn more about those masks later), but I chose to heal! Vulnerability provides me freedom to properly heal, vulnerability provides me comfort in knowing its ok to feel, and vulnerability allows to me to touch countless lives of other tenacious queens every single day.

In our culture, vulnerability has become synonymous with weakness. Yet Dr. Brené Brown has discovered through 12 years of research that vulnerability is not weakness at all, but is our strongest connection to our humanity and to each other. "Vulnerability is the birthplace of love, belonging, empathy, creativity, and authenticity-the experiences that bring meaning to our lives". You cannot selectively numb sections of vulnerability because by default you will numb your joy.

 Time to Slay:

- Who in your life has stifled the expression of your feelings?
- How do you deny yourself an emotional outlet?
- How would it feel to not have to feel to wear the mask anymore?
- What is one step you can take towards healing?

Chapter 6
Shame doesn't have to be Part of your Story

> "Shame is a soul eating emotion." – C.G. Jung

As you begin to expose yourself and remove the layers of masks in your life, shame may come up for you. Merriam Webster define *shame* as a painful emotion caused by consciousness of guilt, shortcoming, or impropriety.

Based on Margaret Paul, PhD insight she shared in one of resources titled: *Inner Bonding*, she shares-"the healing process can only truly begin when we understand and embrace our shame. Shame is the primary emotion responsible for creating and shaping the false selves that develop inside of us and eventually overshadows our being and our purpose. These false selves better known as subpersonalities are really survival roles which we create at first to help us make it in the confusing, complex and double-messaged environment of our family systems. These sub-personalities are warped images of our real nature that help to hide who we really are, they are also the means by which we get our emotional needs met as we know no other way".

Shame feels like you've done something very, very wrong — so wrong that your self-esteem withers and you see yourself as seriously flawed. We often confuse shame with guilt, but they are not the same. As shame and vulnerability author and speaker **Brené Brown** says, "The difference between shame and guilt is the difference between 'I am bad' and 'I did something bad.'"

Sadly, how we were treated by others when we were children becomes the way we internally treat ourselves. Going back to the scene when I was approximately 7 years old, which I was teased that I was crying while watching "The Wizard of Oz" forced me to speak to myself like that at times. I instantly stuffed my feelings down and told that inner child to stop acting like a baby. Over time, the experiences within your environment which we were shamed as a child become the unconscious triggers for feeling and expressing shame as adults. For example, it took me years to feel comfortable to cry in front of people. I was deeply embarrassed and humiliated to cry as early as a teenager. I would do everything in my power to repress feelings that might make me cry. All I heard in my head was the teasing of me crying while watching that emotional movie.

During the early point of our lives, it's very easy to download a belief of shame similar to what happened to me. "As a result of not feeling loved, valued and understood, you can develop the belief that the reason why you were not being loved was because there was something wrong with you. Once the core shame belief is activated, we become addicted to it because now we are blaming ourselves for the action of others. The thought of feeling like we can do something about the situation gives us a "false" sense of power. It's easier to hang on to the thought that our inadequacy is provoking the behavior of others and we don't want to accept our own helplessness over another person feelings and/or behavior.

Shame also protect us from other feelings that we are afraid to feel. Shame gives us control over our own feelings. I have discovered in coaching sessions with many women that they were covering their feeling of shame with heartbreak, sadness, or anger over others. It's hard to accept that shame is a personal feeling caused by your own limiting disbeliefs, but loneliness, grief, or even helplessness over others are all more "accepted" societal feelings. It is common to feel grief if someone passes away. It is common to feel heartbreak if your husband asks for a divorce. It is common to feel lonely when you move to a new demographic location and do not know anyone.

Unfortunately, it's not common to admit that you have a limiting belief of shame. If you are finding it difficult to move beyond shame, it may be because you are addicted to the feeling of control that your shame-based beliefs have given you: Control over others' feelings and behavior, and control over your own authentic feelings. As long as having the control is most important to you, you will not let go of your false core shame beliefs.

If this is you, I give you permission to get past this mindset block by answering some tough questions so that you get to experience freedom and be your authentic self!

 *Time to Slay:*

1. **Revisit your childhood**
    a. What past scenario started the path of shame belief?
2. **Recognize your triggers**
    a. Were you rejected in some way that reminded you of childhood rejection? Were you

caught in looping thoughts about an event that feels shameful?

3. **Practice compassion**
    a. How can you go back to that moment when the shame belief enters your subconscious and heal that person?
    b. What were the words or actions you desperately wanted to hear at that moment which could have prevented the shame cycle?

4. **Accept love and kindness**
    a. Make space in your heart and mind for those who are trying to love you. A person who is dealing with shame can block love or be afraid to love.
    b. Remind yourself daily that you ARE LOVED. Regardless of the child who was abused, forgotten, or mistreated.

5. **Practice forgiveness**

    a. Have a Forgiveness ceremony

When you struggle to forgive yourself, you consequently cannot forgive others. In retrospect, when you cannot forgive others, you cannot forgive yourself. So, the lesson here forgive yourself AND others since the dynamic of forgiveness is the same in both cases.

Not forgiving is like carrying heavy suitcases full of bricks through an airport with no wheels and no shoulder pads. Forgiving is leaving the suitcase and walking away and saying heck to all of the stuff in it. Forgiving opens doors to blessings in your life. You are able to enjoy life, be genuinely happy again, and see the wonderful beauty in all who is around you. Sometimes writing a letter to the person who offended you can help. I wrote a letter to my mother. I tried to talk to her several times in the past as a teenager and there was no opportunity to share my total heart so writing a letter allowed me to release all hurt and pain. I wrote it as if I was speaking to her. It lifted so much pain off my heart and mind. It removed so many mindset blocks I had in my heart for years.

I became a new woman who was unstoppable. Maybe you need to forgive yourself for a few things; you haven't put yourself on the to-do list, you let some goals through the cracks, or been super distracted with goals which resulted in pushing yourself to the side. Maybe there are somethings you are angry with yourself about. Maybe you have said some very hurtful things to yourself.

Do you need a break-through to fully forgive someone or yourself? You can write a letter to yourself, it's time to forgive so that you can began a new chapter of positive communications with self. When you write, this letter prepares an actual ceremony or ritual. You can burn the letter, rip it up, or throw it in a body of water. Come up with something that is symbolic and something that will remind you that you made this new proclamation in your life.

Every time a gremlin comes in with a negative thought that makes you feel guilty, resentful, or emotional disturbing, you will remember that you held a ceremony to "let it go" and on that day, you released it. I am telling you this is a life-changer to move forward. It will constantly remind you of the "New You" and your new chapter.

Chapter 7
Shifting into Royalty Language

> "I allow abundance to flow into me…for I am the divine receptacle for the blessing."
>
> - CJ Reynold

As I mentioned earlier, when I turned 30 years old I began to see life a little different. My daily mission was to create a better *Erica* through dropping the "pawn" mindset and dreaming bigger and believing that whatever I do will be purposeful actions in helping others think better and do better! I am proud to say I am doing that every day!

Let's examine what it means to be a pawn.

Pawn pôn/ noun: pawn; plural noun: pawns
a chess piece of the smallest size and value

Remember the Chess board of life story shared early and how I had my wake-up call? Well, I was done playing small, I was ready to DREAM BIG! Think Big. Believe Big. Act Big. And I've had some BIG results! I've embraced the Queen mentality over my life by letting go of past hurts and pain to step into my inheritance! Now I want to help you.

Pawns sacrifices itself for every piece on the chess board. Sounds familiar? Yes, as women, it's easy to do the same thing. We go about our day and make sure kids are ready for school, spouse has a home cooked meal, house is cleaned, projects completed at work, extended family members assisted with "emergencies". How in the world do we focus on ourselves when SO much is going on? To cultivate the Queen which is already in you; there comes a time to stop thinking as a pawn and start thinking as a Queen! Time to start building a Queen mindset. So instead of putting yourself in a "box" and allowing it to define your ultimate role in life, began to work on self. I am here to give you the tools to empower yourself to shift into royalty language.

It all starts with intentions to mentally step you're your inheritance. In order to achieve ANYTHING in life, you have to imagine yourself already achieving it. You have to picture it in your mind and FEEL the success of accomplishing your goal. Today I want you to believe in yourself and your dreams. Don't think about the "HOW".

You have to be like a child, and have some imagination. Act as if you already have it.

Time to Slay:

- What is stopping you from dropping the "Pawn" mindset?
- What are you prepared to leave behind?
- Are you "hanging onto any baggage" just because it feels comfortable? So many people I talk to are desperate to change themselves, but refuse to let go of the past ... or even the present. Let's face it, to have things be different in your life, you have to do things differently and be different yourself. That means that some "less-than-useful" aspects of yourself must be thrown out.
- What makes it difficult for you to move forward?

Chapter 8
Slay Limiting Thoughts

> "Believe in an abundant universe. Life is proliferating life. Its's scientific fact that there's more where that came from. More love, more genius, more time, more you." – Danielle Laporte

As a black woman, I kept hearing in my head that only white women can earn $5,000 for a 90-day coaching/mentorship package with my private practice. I didn't believe that it could happen for me. I felt like people of my same ethnicity could only afford cheaper prices. Unfortunately, that mindset blocked all types of opportunities in my life and business up until I began to shift into royalty language.

Royalty language focuses on abundance and "pawn" mindset focuses on lack. A scarcity mindset will stop you dead in your tracks on this tenacious journey towards a more abundant and prosperous life. It's essential to get quite acquainted with the language you speak to yourself. Unfortunately, a lot of the time the language we speak to ourselves can be quite negative.

To illustrate the power of language, let's examine Dr. Emoto's water crystal experiment. Dr. Masaru Emoto's water crystal experiments consisted of exposing water in glasses to different words, pictures or music, and then freezing and examining the aesthetic properties of the resulting crystals with microscopic photography. Emoto made the claim that water exposed to positive speech and thoughts would result in visually pleasing crystals being formed when that water was frozen, and that negative intention would yield "ugly" frozen crystal formations.

More than likely before reading this book you already knew that positive and negative thinking have a major impact on the surrounding environment. However, Emotos tangible evidence provides powerful backing to the concept. If the words and thoughts that come out of us have this effect on water crystals, it's amazing to think of what kind of effect your thoughts have on yourself. To further blow your mind, the average human body represents 60% of water.

I challenge you from this day forward to be mindful and reject every negative thought such as, "I can't', "I haven't", "I need", "if', "but" and replace those with: "I CAN", "I WILL", "I HAVE"! As you consistently replace the negative with positive, the negative will have to CEASE!

I recommend journaling your thoughts and reflect back on them as much as you need. Remember our emotions can change by the minute, but those deep dreams you have deep down is what your heart bleeds for each and every day. Don't allow anything or anyone deter you from pursing your life passion; not even yourself. You are a Queen and it's time for you to claim your inheritance!

NO MORE NEGATIVE THOUGHTS! As your mind changes, this builds a great foundation for you to achieve the life you desire and deserve.
We lost our ability to dream because of our own limiting thoughts. But not anymore for you. It's time to change the way you speak to yourself. This will be a moment in your life that requires elevated language with self.

Time to Slay:

Affirmation statements to slay limiting beliefs:

- ✓ I am enough!
- ✓ I am a powerful change agent!
- ✓ I am the epitome of tenacity!
- ✓ I am a trusted friend!
- ✓ I am an intelligent woman!
- ✓ I am ABUNDANT regardless of the size of my bank account!

- Create your own "I AM" statements

- Each day look into the mirror and tell yourself 3 things that you are extremely proud of that girl you see in the mirror has accomplished, share 3 things which you can forgive her for, and share 3 things you will commit to do for her that day. Talk to yourself as if you were a close friend or (even better) your daughter. You will never allow your daughter to have ongoing negative thoughts and you will never allow her to give up on herself. So, do not give up on yourself either! Keep the momentum going!

- Try placing sticky notes around your house with "I Can", "I Will" statements. Every time you see the statements, repeat phrase out loud 3 times. For example, "I can be a successful entrepreneur" "I can live a happy and abundant life", "I will marry the man of my dreams", I will have the bank account I desire". Don't limit your dreams and remember do not think about the how. Have infinite trust that these blessings will show up in your life.

Chapter 9
Silencing the Gremlins

> "Perhaps I am stronger than I think."
> -Thomas Merton

Recently I caught myself shrinking and doubting my dreams and visions. I claimed on my vision board that people would gravitate to me like Lisa Nichols or Oprah. I started shrinking and doubting I would be speaking on a platform with millions of women in the audience. Then a close friend and fellow coach had me say out loud the characteristics and traits of women I look up to and acknowledge that I have those special traits and actually MORE than them in some ways. I INSTANTLY stepped into my power. I repeated to myself, "I am unstoppable. My tenacity is fierce! I am stronger than I think! I WILL be sharing my story and inspiring millions of women. My story is my fuel".

If you are going through one problem after another ... have you thought about if it's YOU that is attracting it? God has given us the power to choose life or death for our journey. If you are in a vicious negative cycle, you can retrain the brain to be more happy, healthy, and prosperous.

> "Happiness is not something you postpone for the future; it is something you design for the present."
> – Jim Rohn

I had a coaching session with a person who had lost over 100lbs THREE times and gained it all back. This time, he gained almost 200lbs. He struggled so much with guilt. Those gremlins were speaking to him every single day, telling he was wasn't worth the effort. He was so mad at himself for dropping the ball on his goals. He was beyond hurt with himself to be able to achieve such a significant goal then return back to past habits and behaviors which placed him at the beginning of his journey in the first place. Maybe you can relate to this man. Have you achieved something so great then took 2-3 steps backwards because of those pesky gremlins? Gremlins are mischievous creatures that don't like bright light, which I refer to as positive thinking. The more you feed your mind positivity the gremlins will disappear. Gremlins come to take joy, create chaos, and will stop you dead in your tracks towards any dream.

You may be in an uncomfortable place within your mindset due to setbacks; each day your past hangs over your head. You walk around with guilt in everything you touch. It's like walking around with a ball and chain strapped to your ankles. You are moving, but boy! It is at a slow dreadful pace. These are some of the hardest emotional traps to get out of. It spills over into how you perform at work, your relationships, and of course your language you speak to yourself on a daily basis.

My client and I had a long first session, but at the end we discovered that he needs to look at his goal as a "project" - a continuance project. Each time he lost the weight he would ask himself, "what's next?" But instead of creating another "project" he would just go back to his old ways. We identified his pattern and were able to create a plan to avoid the pitfall. He also discovered that his "why" is to become a HEALTH COACH himself one day. I told him how powerful his journey would be to help others see that it's ok to "fail"- as long as you fail forward! We both cried tears of joy for his shifted mindset to slay his mindset gremlins. These are the best transformation moments I share with clients and the most meaningful role I ever had in my life. I love being an agent of transformation!

Time to Slay:

- What type of language have you been using with yourself? What are the common pitfalls with your self-talk?

- How is your language affecting your relationship? Work performance? Confidence? Business?

- What are 3 things you can do on a daily basis which will help you slay those pesky gremlins?

Chapter 10
Release Resistance

> "By releasing resistance a little more every day, you will feel the power that creates worlds flowing through you...just breathing and listening, not to make something happen, but for the pleasure and comfort of alignment." - Abraham Hicks

I had so much resistance in my 6th grade science class while a young lady by name the of Sulai continuously talked about Jesus and invited me to her church. She was speaking a very different language than I was used to and she was way too excited about this dude named: Jesus. At that time, I felt like she was telling me about a "fictitious man" and his love for me. All I could do is question; how could he love me? I didn't feel like anyone loved me at that time of my life. My mom and I couldn't have a decent conversation without her yelling at me, claiming I was being disrespectful and I couldn't avoid fist fights with other kids since I always had something to say.

The most confusing aspect of Sulai's interaction with me was we were polar opposites: Her sweet and pleasant demeanor versus my sassy attitude with a chip on my shoulder just didn't add up. We were like oil and water. I was a very angry and frustrated child because I constantly felt limited and misunderstood by everyone. I was the person who would do a lot of talking and basically want to run. However, I had to defend myself which resulted in the constant fist fights.

I was using my gift for gab as the mask to appear as this hard-core person who was actually just really a lonely and sad child seeking attention. I felt segregated most days and very limited. One of my biggest aggravations were the limited opportunities to ride my bike within my neighborhood; I was forced to ride my bike on the top roof of a garage on Martin Luther King Boulevard in Cleveland, Ohio. I couldn't even ride the bike in a straight path for God sake.

I was an 11-year-old girl on a purple and pink 10 speed bike creating figure 8s within a very small space on top of a garage. It was horrible for me and I was teased a lot by the other children in the neighborhood. During this time, I didn't have many friends because I was such a mouthy child who thought she knew it all. Remember when I mentioned at the beginning of the book my identity crisis? Well, because of the masks, I didn't hang out with any particular groups of people because I truly didn't know who I was and what I stood for.

Teachers would constantly contact my mom complaining that I verbally undermined their requests or was always "trying" to be the class clown. Despite my resistance and masks, the young lady in my 6th grade science class was persistent with the invitation to her church. Almost a year later, I eventually said, "yes". Twenty-two years later I am still great friends with Sulai. She will always have a special place in my heart because she invited me to the two most important men of my life: Jesus and my husband Joshua.

As I approached Sulai's church, I was very nervous with sweaty palms, increased heart rate, and a dry mouth. There were thoughts to just to have my mom turn around based on how nervous I felt. I was thinking to myself, why did I allow that girl to talk me into coming to this unknown place who praise a man named *Jesus*? When mom dropped me off at the front of the church on Cooley Ave., I walked into the main area where I was greeted by very friendly ushers. Everyone was nice and loving. It was such a different environment than I was used to. At home, it was constant yelling or complaints, not hugs or happy conversations. I was still at the uncomfortable stage wanting to dart out with quickness, but people kept approaching me to introduce themselves.

Then a goofy man at the time who was the Youth Pastor came and welcomed me to the church and instantly invited me to Youth Camp. I was thinking, "Is he crazy?" I just arrived 15 mins ago, I haven't even sat in the pew yet and experience service. I was still unsure if I was going to stay for the duration of the service. I really didn't say yes, but he eagerly had me fill out some form then sent me across the street where the youth were at for service.

Three guys were standing in the back (one of them was my current husband) and just stared at me as if they never seen a girl before. It was funny and creepy all at the same time. We chatted and made a few jokes as they explained to me how the services worked including extracurricular activities the youth were involved in. The conversation with the guys actually helped me get more comfortable and excited to be in this new environment.

When I reflect back on this story it dawned on me that the crazy Youth Pastor DID sign me up for Youth Camp. This is when my life changed, my resistant walls began to fall and I started allowing love in my heart. The church became my second family. Each week I grew stronger and stronger and open my heart more and more.

From the time, I first attended youth camp in 1999 up until now, I have removed many layers of resistance in my life. As I grew in my professional and personal life, each level would reveal deeply ingrained gremlins of resistance. I didn't connect the dots and realize the level of impact resistance had played in my capacity to receive until I stumbled across a phenomenal group of women led by a Transformational Coach via Facebook. She shared her story about how her life had changed when she relinquished resistance to expand her capacity to receive. What I learned from her is that resistance usually takes the form of subconscious fear and doubts, which prevents our desires from manifesting into our life.

That caught my attention and it was such impeccable timing for me since I was just starting to have thoughts about how much more I could have in life if I would release the baggage and walk in confidence. I signed up for her FREE 5-day course and I was blown away by the countless blessings and clarity I started to receive. I started to see sequence numbers like crazy which were confirmations that I was on track. I have learned on my journey that God speaks to me in many different ways: through a person, a message, a song, situations, and even through angel numbers. Angel numbers are a way for your celestial guides to communicate with you.

They can deliver specific messages through certain numbers or number sequences. This communication most often manifests in a series of repeat numbers or a series of synchronistic numbers. For example, it has been times I am looking at the clock and seeing 11:11 or checking out at the grocery store with $33.33. Seeing these numbers is one of the most common ways for angels to let you know they are present, because numbers are a universal language.

When you keep seeing the same numbers at seemingly just the "right" moment, your guides are calling you to explore the vibrational significance of those numbers. They are giving you a gentle nudge to quiet your mind and reflect on those numbers, their purpose, their meaning, and their message. And the more a number repeats in sequence, the more "supercharged" its vibration becomes. Once your angels have gotten your attention, ask them if they have anything more to tell you. Meditate and invite the angels into your space.

Based on Doreen Virtue's best-selling book, Angel Numbers 101 shares there is a range of numbers that have each been assigned a specific meaning. This range includes the numbers 1-9, and the master numbers 11 and 22. Where their meanings came from is a mystery. But the study of angel numbers and the study of numerology dates back thousands of years ago.

> 0 – You are receiving divine guidance and reassurance on your path.

1 – Keep your thoughts positive, focus on your desires and suppress your fears. Your thoughts create reality.

2 – Stay optimistic and continue to hold the vision, even through tough times.

3 – Your guides are with you offering love and wisdom.

4 – Your angels are surrounding you to offer assistance in this exact moment.

5 – Positive change is coming. Ask your angels to help you manifest this change.

6 – Release fear, embrace trust, and find balance between the spiritual and material realms.

7 – Your path is aligned with Divine fortune. Pay attention to new opportunities.

8 – Infinite success and abundance are yours, in alignment with your Higher Purpose.

9 – It is time to begin the work of your Soul Path, now that you have all you need.

11 – Your intuition is on target. Keep your thoughts and vision aligned with your intention and your greatest dreams.

22 – Be patient, your prayers have been received and will soon be realized if you continue to work towards them.

Apart from seeing these numbers every day, I won and obtained thousands of dollars' worth of gifts which all of them were to help me grow my vision. I began claiming that I will be on a large platform speaking to millions of women sharing my story and inspiring them to be unstoppable. I had a dream of me on the stage with other powerhouse leaders in the industry encouraging over 1000 women. I saw myself standing with Lisa Nichols, Oprah, and Steve Harvey backstage getting ready and we were speaking as if we were friends. I really started believing.

Typically, I don't share those things because I normally would think someone would be jealous or doubt. But I dropped that resistance and I am sharing with you today. People have encouraged me and confirm that they do see these visions as well.
Remember everything is energy. What you resist will persist in your life. You have to expand your capacity to receive and see yourself worthy to have it all! The biggest thing with resistance is believing you deserve the dream to happen in your life.

> "Push yourself to do more and to experience more. Harness your energy to start expanding your dreams. Yes, expand your dreams. Don't accept al life of mediocrity when you hold such infinite potential within the fortress of your mind. Dare to tap into your greatness." -Robin S. Sharma

Time to Slay:

- Are you masking your pain? Are you resistant to allowing yourself to be vulnerable due to past hurts and heartache?

- How can you drop the resistance in your life?

- What are those resistance gremlins saying in your head? Are they telling you to not dream big? Are they saying, who do you think you are dreaming this big"?

- You have to believe your dreams can happen you cannot doubt one second that your biggest dreams can be fulfilled.

Chapter 11
Journey to Self-Love

> "Document the moments you feel most in love with yourself- what you're wearing, who you're around, what you're doing. Recreate and repeat."
> - Warsan Shire

The first thought a person has when they hear the word *tenacity* is something associated with external movement or force. Like discussed several times in this book, tenacity is continuance self-improvement. All of tenacious behavior stems from the condition of our heart. When we start removing the layers of blocks in our lives we are able to move tenaciously on our paths. As women, we tell our spouse, kids, and family members that we love them, but do we even love ourselves?

If you hate yourself, it would be difficult if not impossible to love others. You cannot give out to someone what you cannot even do for you. If you don't love yourself because you think that you are too bad of a person or that you are not good enough, "if only people knew the real you". Then it's the same way that you love other people. Anyone that you perceive is not good enough or that they are too "bad" of a person, will not be showed love by you. This is the order that God set things in motion.

The first thing I would like for you to do is learn your love language. Have you taken this test before? Do you know your own love language?

Here are the categories as stated in Dr. Gary Chapman's book, The 5 Love Languages:

- **Words of Affirmation** (kinds words, notes, affirming words),
- **Acts of Service** (helping with chores, serving anytime something needs to be done),
- **Receiving Gifts** (loves to give spontaneous gifts, especially when visiting or if they went on a trip somewhere),
- **Quality** Time (sharing undivided attention with each other, could be in person or on the phone, as long as conversation is happening uninterrupted),
- **Physical Touch** (being touched lovingly and on purpose, hugs)

Which one do you gravitate to more? Now that you know your Love Language you can start LOVING yourself! You can also take the Love Language profile assessment provided to you in the "Time to Slay" at the end of chapter to learn more about your language. If you like to receive gifts…go get yourself a gift. If you like Acts of Service hire someone to help you on a project or household chores. If you like Physical Affection…get a massage. You get what I am saying? LOVE YOURSELF FIRST. Don't just expect people to do these things for you. Do them for yourself FIRST!

A mother loves her newborn child without reservation, and romantic love, in its first stages of infatuation, can make the beloved seem perfect. But most of us doubt that love without reservation, love completely forgiving and accepting, exists in our everyday lives. Looking in the mirror, all of us see too many flaws and remember too many past wounds and failings to love ourselves without also putting a limit on that love. Let's take the limits off today!

What's keeping you from loving yourself unconditionally? I suggest you journal your thoughts so that you can reflect back on them at a later day and see your progress towards healing.

We live in a world where there is an epidemic of low selfesteem. It affects almost every aspect of our lives, from how we think about ourselves to the way we think about or react to life situations. When negative influences and thoughts are prevalent — generated either from within ourselves or through others — it adversely affects the way we feel about ourselves. It also affects the experiences we have in our lives.

Think about it in terms of nurturing your children. When they do something, you don't want them to do, you don't just hate them or disown them; you love them unconditionally.

Your body needs this same type of love you display to your children as well. The more you love your current body the more it works with you to achieve your desired goal. People think a weight loss journey is all about nutrition and fitness. I'm here to help you see that your mindset is a critical piece to lose weight.

Over time this can lead to low self-esteem which can reduce the quality of a person's life in many different ways. Unchecked, low self-esteem may even lead to mental health issues such as anxiety and depression, sometimes with tragic results.
Body image and self-esteem go hand in hand. When you look in the mirror, how do you feel?
Are you saying mean things? Having regrets? Feeling frustrated?

Shift Your Perspective Focus on:

- What your body can do
- How good it feels to be healthy
- All the things you can do because of your body

Chances are you say mean things to yourself when you look in the mirror. Every day pick a piece of your body you absolutely love and show it off with pride. Did you know your high intense emotion of "hate" towards your body can slow down weight loss progress?

Knowing your love language gives you confidence, you can now communicate with others on how they can love you better. You are the CEO of your life. You do not have to accept ANY type of love. Also, remember to treat yourself as the Queen which is your birth right and inheritance which we discussed earlier in the book.

Time to Slay:

- Take the Love Language Assessment Here: http://www.5lovelanguages.com/profile/

- How will you fill up your self-love tank from the knowledge you learned today?

- What are you willing to commit to from the list of 5 love languages for yourself this week? Who else will benefit?

- What do you need in order to succeed?

- How will you ensure you continuously love yourself FIRST?

Chapter 12

Drop F.E.A.R – (False Evidence Appearing Real)
Art Martin, PhD, *Transform your Mind*

> *"You gain strength, courage and confidence by every experience in which you really stop to look fear in the face. You are able to say to yourself, 'I have lived through this horror. I can take the next thing that comes along.' You must do the thing you think you cannot do."*
> -Eleanor Roosevelt

Fear is one of the conditions of the heart that will stop a person from moving even an inch on their tenacious journey. All of the other concepts we have discussed so far can be compartmentalized and will eventually block your progress to move forward. However, if you are fearful and need to control everything you won't be moving very far on this journey. Any unknown venture, path, or goal requires you to leap! Writing this book was a big leap of faith. I officially unveiled my mask I have been wearing for years and became very vulnerable to you, my reader. Yes, I could easily shrink and fear how some people will view me after reading this book, or how my parents may not be too happy about exposing their past experiences. I can't allow those things to hold me back. I know this book has such a grand purpose and mission to help women unmask themselves and claim their throne.

> **"Fear is nothing, but love upside down."**
> **- Unknown**

I had a privilege to coach a woman who had a fear of speaking in front of large groups of people. Her resistance was pretty strong, it took us several sessions to discover how this same fear was showing up in her relationships, work productivity, and self-worth. Once this was determined it was easy to see the correlation of how control flooded her life. She felt like she had to control everything as early as 11 years old. Her home environment was chaotic and begin controlling things within her reach to soothe and comfort herself in the mist of chaos. As she begins to give herself permission to let go and heal the 11year-old self which led to her controlling ways, her life started transforming.

Your mind's job is to protect YOU. Anything unknown (including success) is scary to it. To keep you safe it will do just about anything to make you listen to it.

Think about what you are fearful of? I bet it's something that you don't like or something unknown to you, isn't it? **One of the best** ways to transform fear is to convert it into self-love. The foundation which stems from the confidence you have in yourself and your abilities. This all can accomplished through consistently using royalty language so that your love creates an unstoppable YOU!

Here are different types of fear:

- Fear of failure,
- Fear of the unknown,
- Fear of public speaking
- Fear due to anxiety,
- Fear of starting your own business,
- Fear of being vulnerable
- Fear of rejection

> **"Always go with the choice that scares you the most, because that's the one that is going to help you grow." -Caroline Myss**

Isn't it amazing how children have a care-free attitude? This is because they do not have any impressions. As we grow up we gather a stock of good and bad experiences. Start addressing where the fear came from and start removing layers from there.

Time to Slay:

- Are you acting on faith or fear? If you weren't scared, what would you do?
- If you changed your belief about FEAR, what would be possible? What does this mean to you?
- Face the anxiety with strength – Use fear as guidance about what you go after since it's an indicator to about the things you deeply care about and your truest desire. When you are feeling scared

or anxious, a few minutes of breath work comes in handy and provides clarity (4-7-8 Plan)—Take in deep breath in for 4 seconds, hold for 7 secs, then release for 8 secs

- What's the worst that can happen if you step into your "fear zone"? Can you handle it?

SECTION 2: CREATE THE VISION

Chapter 13

Tapping into your Inner Child

> "The kid in you holds the key to living a full and rich life. Let her out to play." - Cheryl Richardson

I had a peculiar environment as a child. I don't remember ever playing with toys or Barbie dolls. What I do remember is being alone a lot in the projects on Hough Avenue in Cleveland, Ohio left to survive on my own. One of my childhood highlights were remembering my wonderful deceased Godfather bringing my mom and I Chinese food in the middle of the night. However, I don't remember a time of using my imagination until I was approximately 11 years old.

Unfortunately, my mom was addicted to drugs up until I was 6 years old, I didn't feel free or safe to have a full imagination. It wasn't a time for care-free adventure or playful exploration. I was young and I had no option but to save and protect myself. I am so glad that my mom changed her life completely around when the court threatened to give my aunt 100% custody over me. Anything prior to that timeframe is such a blur. I blocked it out, because sometimes we block things out to have the strength to keep going. When people say, "think back to the time you were a child," I think about my pre-teenage years, years when I felt protected and safe enough to imagine, create and play. My sister, a friend of the family, and I would take the slide and pillow to create gladiator obstacle courses. Remember the show Gladiators in the 1990s? We were inspired by the show and created so many courses with only two items (a slide and pillow). We didn't completely mimic the 1990s TV show events such as Power Ball, Assault, or the Wall, but we creatively created obstacles which we had to climb over the slide or under the slide dodging house furniture within a certain timeframe using a stop watch.

We played for hours at a time and we laughed so hard when we would fall and trip while running through our homemade obstacle courses. We also created our own rap cassette tapes. Yes, cassette tapes. That feels like so long ago. Remember TLC? I was T-Boz, my 6-year-old younger sister was Chilly, and our friend of the family was left-eye. We sang those songs like we were singing for a sold-out show at Fox Theatre in Atlanta. We listened to the recordings and critiqued ourselves until we felt like it was ready to "publish". To whom? We didn't know; however, we were imagining, dreaming, and having so much fun.

Remember when you played as a child, you explored every small rock, played with the box that your toy came in, used your fingers to dig through dirt and grass, and ran without a worry about time or purpose or direction?

Remember when everything around you were novel and effortless, filled with joy? Dreaming and imagining was the only way you knew how to think and explore life.
Did you ever play with dolls and imagine Ken was your husband and you would reenact your interpretation of what a "relationship" or "marriage" supposed to look like? Recently, I was observing my 5-year-old nephew and his imagination is out of this world! He has the Peppa Pig and

friend's deluxe house set. He tucked himself under the dining room table at my in-law's home after he asked several of us to play with him with his new toy set. The home was crowded with approximately ten of us and there was so much noise around him. We were all having our own conversations. You know what I mean, 2-3 people on one side of the house talking about sports, a few people in the kitchen discussing the Thanksgiving menu and some in the living room discussing family drama.

For those who can relate, there was also a person who was passed out on the reclining chair in the living room with the TV watching him. However, the laughter and chatter didn't distract my nephew's mission to enact his imagination. I sat back in the corner of the living room against their piano as I gazed in amazement on how he was able to create a scene of 6 people on his own. I chuckled a few times because he was intensely engaged with his imagination. If I would had told him that everything he was doing just pretend or not true, he would have probably yelled at me in disbelief and think I was the "crazy" one. That is how convinced he was of the scene he had set up and was acting out.

He had provided names for all the characters and their roles in life. All by himself he created a whole scene of them playing outside the home which my husband and his mom helped him build earlier that day. My nephew claimed that Peppa the Pig was very angry with his friends. He spoke in different tones so that everyone had their own personality which by the way matched their outfits somehow. He was content, happy, free, and open! Of course, watching him made me think about how can we adults live more like the young imaginative boy playing with Peppa the Pig and friends deluxe house set under the table?

Unfortunately, the demands of our lives - work, family, money, health- causes us to gradually lose that sense of wonder. Our imagination is stifled by reality; it's a little more challenging for us to dream and see the impossible as possible. We are almost scared to think happy thoughts thinking it will attract bad things to happen because someone taught us about "Murphy's Law" and now it's embedded into our subconscious mind. You know the law: anything that can go wrong, will go wrong. With this mindset, it's very tough to feel free to imagine or even dream about a goal to achieve. Throughout this chapter I want to help you remove the layers in your mind so that you feel free, motivated, and confident to dream. Even if you didn't have a great childhood and/or can't recall that feeling of being like my nephew, or like myself when I was 11 years old.

What I want to show you is that even if your childhood was dark or a big blur, it doesn't prevent you from tapping into your inner child. That inner child is in there somewhere; we may have to tug a bit to get her to come out and play. However, once you learn the secret to unlocking the doorway to your inner child, it will help you create vivid and clear visions for yourself and your life. The clearer the vision, the higher the chances it will manifest into your life. It's imperative to release yourself from the cycle of being so serious and take time to pause and allow our minds to wonder. Your imagination is not lost forever; it's just buried underneath layers of disappointments and real life trauma and pain. We can learn a lot from a child. Let's reflect on specific moments of your childhood. Explore who you were when you were happiest, most confident, and think about what you enjoyed as a child.

How do we translate the intrinsic and valuable qualities of playfulness into adulthood? How can play, imagination, curiosity and invention be a part of every day? As an adult, you can reconnect to the playful spirit and untapped source of energy that are your birthright when you embrace these simple tools in your life. I recommend you start incorporating these 10 thoughts into your life so that you allow your inner child to be released and maximize your experiences in life:

Time to Slay:

1. Play

How can you play more in life? I know my "play" tank is a big one to fill. I constantly have to have moments to let down my guard as an adult and have a couple of drinks to have fun with hubby or family/friends. The way I play is dancing or singing. Our favorite spot is the Cleveland Big Bang where you can go and have the songs you request played so you can sing along. Ellen, the comedian and TV show host, is another great example of someone who incorporates play in her daily segment as she comes out on the stage playing a song and showing off her dance moves during the talk show "The Ellen Show". When Ellen comes down the aisles she is being herself—her playful, creative self, dancing for the sheer fun of it. It is so cool to see the audience joining in and dancing with her. Each day her fans anticipates her dance ritual and her form of "play" to continue. Dancing at the start of the show has become her signature—a way for Ellen to connect with her audience. Her carefree individual style of play has given others the permission to do the same.

2. Try New Things

The brains of babies and toddlers are "plastic," explains Alison Gopnik, author of The Philosophical Baby: What Children's Minds Tell Us about Truth, Love, and the Meaning of Life and a professor of psychology and affiliate professor of philosophy at the University of California at Berkeley. That means babies are constantly making new connections and constantly learning. Exposing yourself to new activities — can actually induce brain plasticity. This expands our brain to have the ability to learn and modify our behavior.
When you put yourself in unfamiliar situations you are trying things are new to you. I encourage you to learn a language, try an instrument you've always wanted to play or hit the road and travel to a new place. New wires (neural pathways) which give instructions to our bodies are activated and opens up our pathways to think clearer and minimize brain fog so that it's easier to dream and use your imagination.

3. "Explore" Instead of Solving

It's very easy as adults to focus on the "solve" component of a problem instead of exploring. Children are constantly exploring different possibilities to learn for the sake of learning. As adults, we are focused on learning with a clear concise "end-goal" or purpose. When we try new things simply for the sake of trying new things, it forces us to think in different ways.

4. Find a Hobby

How are you sparking your joy on a daily basis? When I ask a client this question, they stare back at me like a deer caught in the headlights. Most adults are not sparking joy in their life on a daily basis. As adults, it's become easy to focus on work, errands, and household tasks without engaging in an activity which brings joy to your heart for at least 5-10 minutes a day. For years, I went into different circles trying to figure out a hobby. I encourage you to engage an activity which brings pure happiness to you for a small amount of time each day and watch the magic happen. "When we ignite more creative experiences in our life, we channel our inner child," says Gabrielle Bernstein, author of Miracles Now, "Creativity offers us freedom to be ourselves and let loose!"

5. Count the Small Blessings

Kids have a way of being excited about the smallest things. Such as going on road trip to Sam's club, having a sleep over at your house, or able to stay outside past the time street lights come on. Oprah says, "Be thankful for what you have and you'll end up having more". Take a look at your life and count the smallest blessings or as Lisa Nichols says it, "micro-wins".

6. Spend time with kids

As I did with my nephew, take time to observe a child while they are in their most imaginative state. It will teach you a lot about how to expand your mind and see life through a different lens.

7. Live life in a Mindful way

When you live a life in continuance mindfulness, you are living life in the moment. When a child is at his/her full imaginative state, they are not thinking about what is going to happen or the consequences. They are putting all of their energy into the now. In the present moment, you can truly experience life. I recommend that you bring your attention to your breaths as you naturally breathe. As you walk a short distance pay attention to how your body reacts to each movement and how your feet/legs feel as you step.

8. Do something "just because"

Children are free-spirited and do things just because. Have you ever asked a child why they did something? The first answer you will most likely get is "I don't know". They act and do things without a specific reason. Typically, they allowed their heart to move them in that particular path. I know this is hard for my control-freaks. Because essentially you need to know why you are doing anything in your life. I challenge you to release the control a bit and do something at minimal once a week "just because". Dance, watch that TV show you've been waiting to see, or go see a friend, just because.

9. Take time to look around and explore your territory

There is so much to explore around us. Children take time to connect with what is around them with the 5 main senses. They pause long enough to look at the various colors surrounding them, smell what is in the air, see what is in front of them, feel the textures of things within reach, and listen to the different sounds in the area. Take a cue from children who are pros at relishing their surroundings, and pause sporadically to check out everything that is happening around you.

10. Give permission to be YOU

Enough with diluting yourself or censoring your actions. It's time to be unapologetically you. Eliminating the thoughts and concerns of what others think can help with this step in a great way. Laugh when you want to laugh. Cry when you feel the need to cry. Speak out about topics you feel need to be addressed. I believe that we each have the individual responsibility to bring forth our authentic selves into the world.

Chapter 14
You Can Have It All

> "Dream about your IDEAL life. Focus on it until you know exactly what it looks like. Then wake up and do at least one thing every day to make it a reality." – Unknown

For many years, I had a very hard time tapping into the realm of believing ANYTHING was possible for me to achieve. I kept subconsciously attaching the "how" to the equation. With that mindset, I blocked myself from fully dreaming about a limitless ideal life. If a goal wasn't a few steps within reach, then I didn't believe it could happen. Any time a dream would pop up in my mind, all I could think about was my current resources: whether it was money, time or tools. Typically, the conclusion would be that I didn't have enough funds to purchase something, enough time to get things done, or the perfect tools to make my dreams happen. Can you relate?

Within the last few years, I have been uncovering the layers preventing me from thinking outside my own box. The common denominator which was preventing me to adopt the "I can have it all" mentality was the phrase, "I am not good enough". This phrase hunts a lot of us on a daily basis and stops all movement on a journey for a person. Most think the mindset "I am not enough" stems from people searching and searching for more and more in life. However, that same mindset can also make a person feel like they are not worthy to receive anything great in their life and they should stay in poverty, not be happy, or constantly be in lack. If you were raised similar to me, then you will relate with the latter scenario of "not enough" syndrome.

There came a point in my life when I had to ask myself the following question, "How do I want to live daily?" From the time, I wake up until the time I lay my head down on my fluffy goose feathered pillow. When I relinquished the "how" of achieving goals that is when I was born into life all over again. Freely dreaming and tapping into that inner child who doesn't care about "how" things come into reality.

One day I came across Bob Proctor's quote: "Anyone that ever accomplished anything, did not know how they were going to do it. They only knew they were going to do it". Talk about a perfect quote to remind me to drop the "how" regarding a dream. His quote gave me the exact confidence I needed to expand my mind into the ocean of limitless imagination.

I began to research more about Bob Proctor and came across the best-selling self-help book "The Secret" by Rhonda Byrne. Wow, I was blown away. The messages truly changed how I dreamt about goals. Especially the story about how John Assaraf made a vision board with the house he wanted to live in and a few years later he came across that vision board to find the house he was currently living in matched the house he originally placed on the board. When John placed a picture of his dream home on the board, he didn't over-consume himself with "how" he was going to purchase it or what business ventures he would need to be able to afford the home. He simply allowed himself to dream and feel the moment as he walked in the home in amazement.

I was motivated and began to make my first virtual vision board via Oprah's Dream Board website: www.dreamitalive.com. I placed things on there that felt like a stretch and I didn't have a clue on "how" it was going to manifest into my life. I was engulfed in being like a kid in a candy store searching for things I desired and would love to see in my life. A few highlights I put on my vision board were that I desired to earn $10,000 per month with a Health & Wellness business and do a fitness photoshoot. Some months later, I was contacted by a national magazine, Health (www.health.com), to be in their Sept 2014 issue regarding my 65lb weight loss story and some months after my issue was published I hit my first 5figure month as a full-time entrepreneur. Give it a try, it's fun when you let go of limiting beliefs.

Recently, Steve Harvey shared a challenge to write down 500 dreams you have for your life. Yes, 500. Some people can't think of 25. I began to feel stuck at the 200th dream. I truly appreciate this exercise because it forces you to dig really deep in every component of your life. I had a privilege to lock myself in a hotel for a weekend to get this done and it felt amazing to take micro layers of my life and dissect the intentions I expect to see in my life at some point. This painted a very clear vivid picture on how I want to live. This is how I structured the exercise to make it more organized and concise to reach the goal 500 dreams:

Relationships ~
I had to examine the relationships I want present in my life. How do I want my marriage? What quality of sex life do I desire? What type connection do I want with my husband? How do I want us to handle conflict? How many kids do I want? What type of connection do I want with my children? How do I want the pregnancy to be? How do I want the labor to be? What

impact will the kids be on my marriage? What type of friends do I desire in my life? Who are mentors and what role do I want them to play in my aspirations? What type of impact do I want to have on social media? Associates? Friends? Who do I want to help? How do I want to encourage others? How do I want to be mentored? What type of information & chemistry I want exchanged among peers?

Finances ~
What type of income do I want my home to acquire? Where do I want the income to come from? How do I want to bring income within the home? How much do I want to work to achieve my income goal? Who do I want to serve to make income? Will my income come entrepreneurial efforts or salary? How much money do I expect to earn annually, monthly, weekly, hourly, or even by the minute? How much of my income will be profit vs. investment? What type of mindset is required to meet target income? What type of fun do I want to experience with my prosperity level? What type of legacy I want to leave for my children? What type of philanthropic endeavors will I participate in? What type of gifts will I purchase for myself? What luxuries will I indulge in?

Recreational ~
What type of vacations will I take? How will I spend my playtime? How will I ensure work/life balance? How do I want to feel each day when I work? Will it be ease and flow within my life? What type of transportation will I use to travel?

Spirituality ~
What belief systems do I want in place for myself and my family? How will I participate in that system? Who will I want to partner with or what places will I attend to connect others who have the same belief system? What daily rituals will I participate

in so that I continue to grow and evolve as a person? What personal development tools will I use? How will I keep myself accountable?

Health & Wellness ~
What type of energy do I desire? What type of stamina is required to keep up with the life I've envisioned for myself? How do I want to feel in your body? How do I want my external features to look like? How will I ensure I am on track and staying accountable? What mechanisms do I need to have in place to ensure I am setting myself up for success? Who do I need to hire to make it all possible? How do I need my home set-up in order to make health & wellness a priority? What type of mindset is required to put myself on top of the to-do list? If you can answer all of these questions, I am confident you will your goal of 500 dreams!

Time to Slay:

- What are some of your dreams? Use the guideline above to dive in deeper. Also, use
    Oprah's virtual vision board on
    www.dreamitalive.com

- Take time to ask yourself these 3 questions:
    1. Why? Why do you want to achieve this dream? What does these accomplishments mean to you?
    2. Why do you think you don't deserve to obtain this dream?

3. Who do you need to become to achieve your dreams?
4. Why not you? Take this moment to slay limiting thoughts and replace with royalty language.

Chapter 15
The Power of Visualization

> "Visualize: The most amazing life imaginable to you.
> Close your eyes and see it clearly. Then hold the vision for as long as you can…and consider it done."
> – Marianne Willamson

Our brains are powerful mechanisms. As you begin to dream about the life you desire for yourself, I want to help you see how visualization can help take your thoughts of achieving a goal and see it come into manifestation. Let's analyze what happens at a scientific level when we visualize the future.

There are two parts of our brain which are activated when visualizing—the conscious and the subconscious. The conscious part of the brain is the part we are aware of; the here and now. The conscious brain focuses on one thing at a time, whatever we think is most valid and important at the moment. Remember when I explained to you about how I was obsessed with the "how" of achieving a goal? Well, that was my conscious brain stimulants kicking into high gear.

The subconscious brain works a bit different, it sees a complete picture of everything happening all at once. The subconscious mind is aware of everything while the conscious is only aware of certain things.

John Assaraf, Spiritual Entrepreneur & multi-millionaire explains in his documentary, "Train your Brain: The Neuroscience of Financial Success", the differences between conscious and subconscious brain stimulations:

Your conscious brain...

- The amount of information your conscious brain processes is about one-half of the one-millionth of one percent of the amount your subconscious brain processes.
- For all its brilliance, the conscious brain has a major weakness—follow through.
- The conscious brain is great at imagining things and thinking them through, but it's next to useless when it comes to actually getting things done.
- Your conscious brain is amazing at coming up with ideas, but useless when it comes to carrying them out because it is easily distracted. The average person changes focus every six to 10 seconds.
- Goal-setting is something your conscious brain can do.

Your subconscious brain...

- 95% of your behavior is based on subconscious thoughts.
- The subconscious brain can remember billions of things in perfect sequence, not only for minutes at a time, but for your lifetime. How often does it get distracted? Never.

- Goal-attaining is something only your subconscious can do.

You think dreaming about your intentions and visualizing your success before it appears are meaningless efforts? Recent Brain studies now reveal that thoughts produce the same mental instructions as actions does at the cognitive level. Visualization impacts many cognitive processes in the brain: motor control, attention, perception, planning, and memory. So, the brain is getting trained for actual performance during visualization. It's been found that mental practices can enhance motivation, increase confidence and self-efficacy, improve motor performance, prime your brain for success, and increase states of flow – all relevant to achieving your best life and attracting it to appear in your life.

Furthermore, another study published in the Journal of Sport & Exercise Psychology in 2012 examined brain patterns in weightlifters and found that the patterns activated when a weightlifter lifted hundreds of pounds were similar to the brain activations when weightlifters were only thinking about lifting. In some cases, research has revealed that mental practices are almost effective as true physical practice.

As you can see, visualizations are powerful and the key component to activating your dreams. The most importance aspect of visualization is consistent practice. When you visualize, use the 1st person perspective. This is a very important point in manifesting your dreams. First person perspective will be far more powerful than third person, because it is through the first person view that you will live this imagined reality.

Here are key points on how to successfully visualize your dreams into reality:

Train the Brain
By "taking in the good" of your experiences and by imagining, absorbing and enriching the feelings of past, present or future success, you are literally changing the way your brain operates, and becoming a more positive person. The more positive you are the more goodness you attract into your life. Spend time practicing the feeling of achieving your goals- perhaps cultivating the sense of pride, accomplishment, contentment and happiness. This is powerful inner mastery work and as well as profound brain transformation work.

Visualize with FEELING
As you learned, the conscious brain is great at goalsetting and subconscious is great at goal attaining. Thinking about and visualizing a goal is just the beginner's level of visualization. The most important aspect of visualizing your life is to see it in the form vivid pictures which are connected to you in an emotional way. The people who achieve the most are the passionate ones. That passion stems to their emotional connection to their vision. Feeling is the main difference between a person who is static vs. a person who is actually achieving greatness. When you are a pro visualizer, you use the power of emotions. You will maximize your results 10x by adding the elements of FEELING to your mental projections. Research has shown that imaging combined with intense emotion create projections that can stay locked in our memories for

our lifetime. So, visualize using all of your senses (sight, taste, touch, sound, and smell).

Create a Consistent Ritual

Allocate 5-10 mins each day to journal your visions. This is powerful technique and I have personally seen some mind-blowing shifts in my life by adopting this ritual in my life. I written down in present tense that I met powerful mentors, earned a certain amount of money, and had unique experiences. Then it really happens in my life. For example, one year I wrote a check to myself in the amount I desired to make for the upcoming year in the amount of $100,000. I didn't attach the "how" to the situation or analyze the desire. I wrote it down and put the check away in my safe. Sixtydays within the year ending something dawned on me to add up how much was earned that year and by my surprise I had already surpassed the total: $102,365.10. Thoughts truly become things and I was very consistent on my daily visualization rituals.

John Assaraf recommends the best time to visualize is right after you wake or before you go to sleep. These timeframes has been known to be more powerful times to infuse your subconscious with a desired reality. What we feed our consciousness with those high-vibe moments between sleep and conscious states, can literally reprogram our mind and create our desired future.

In addition, practicing visualization directly after meditation will create more powerful results, because during meditation you are more tuned in with your subconscious mind.

After you have completed your visualization rituals, get back to the present moment in with the knowledge of knowing your subconscious has absorbed your desires.

Visualization + Action=RESULTS If you do what you've always done, you'll will be stuck with the same results. There are amazing things that can happen when we understand the science of our brains and begin to visualize our success. However, we can't 100% rely on these concepts and not take action in our lives. That's like a person who gets bariatric surgery. Relying on this surgery will not accomplish positive long-term results. The person still needs to educate themselves on nutrition and even exercise to maximize success and maintain results.

Find your Visualization Flow

Visualization is not necessarily just the art of seeing your goal completely in your mind. Each one of us are wired differently and your visualization flow may not have resonated with another person's preference. Every individual is hard-wired to be dominantly auditory, visual or kinesthetic learners. Take some time and get clear on your way of learning. Some people find it very difficult to visualize, and some use other sensory experience such kinesthetic imagery (imagining touch, movement and feelings). If you are struggling to visualize your goals, don't give up. Write them down. Spend time by yourself, in silence working to bring these goals to life in the way that is best for you to see and feel your dreams.

Time to Slay:

- What emotional connection will you attach to your goals?

- I recommend you document the transformation in your journal. Each day write down your limiting thoughts, your successes, and write out your ideal life experience each day (yes, every single day). Writing out your ideal life can be as simple as a few paragraphs explaining something you would hope to experience or obtain (in the present tense) it's not the same topic each day. You will write whatever you see yourself achieving or experiencing in your mind that day. I recommend you take 1015mins and do this. Here is an example, "Today was amazing! I'm just returning from a conference in Europe which I was the keynote speaker and was publicly recognized for my recent New York Best Selling author award on *Unstoppable Tenacity*". Do you see how I am writing in present tense and just explaining something cool I would like to experience? This exercise allows you to get in the vibration feelings of achieving that success. You don't worry about the how or other details. It's important to totally desensitize logic from the whole experience. This is a moment to use your imagination as if you were 8 years old again.

- I recommend journaling your thoughts and reflect back to them as much as you need. Remember our emotions can change by the minute, but those deep dreams you have deep down are what your heart bleeds for each and every day. Don't allow anything or anyone deter you from pursing your life passion; not even yourself. You are a Queen and it's time for you to claim your inheritance!

Chapter 16
Break the Complacency Curse

> "The tragedy of life is often not in our failure, but rather in our complacency; not in our doing too much, but rather in our doing too little; not in our living above our ability, but rather in our living below our capacities." - Benjamin E. Mays

Sometimes tapping into our inner child and visualization will not really get a person moving on their journey towards their goals. With the hustle and bustle of life, sometimes doing nothing can be a breath of fresh air at times and sometimes that breath of fresh air becomes a week, month, a year, or even decades. *"Complacency is easy...and it is a deadly foe of spiritual growth,"* said Aiden Wilson Tozer. It's very tempting to just settle with what's on your plate than take the necessary steps to create the life you really want. I am guilty of this mindset as well and then realized I was allowing complacency to creep in, diluting my potential and success.

You probably won't believe this story I am about to share or think I am crazy after I explain how my purpose was confirmed and the wake-up call for me to break the complacency curse came into play. I was scrolling through my Facebook newsfeed one day and one of those silly games came across titled: "Get a personalized note about you." You know those Facebook games you basically play by submitting into cyber space some psychic reading or something? Well, I would never think one of them could be so life-changing for me and such an on-time message. I accepted Facebook to produce a "this is a note about you" and wow! I cried. Here is what it said:

> *"A note about Erica: She is crazy because she follows her heart. She believes in taking chances and risking it all for something she truly believes in. We need more and more people like her, for the desires of her heart causes a flame that can ignite so many other beautiful minds. She is one of a kind. She's magic. She knows her worth and what difference she can make with her existence. She perspires herself and inspires others in the process."*

This was my confirmation that I became complacent and it was time for me to step into my ultimate calling and purpose.

I began to see how complacent I had become with my salary role as a Health Coach. Which I love and appreciate. However, I realized I had more to offer to the world. This book was one of the vehicles to make major impact in the world which I continue to serve in my passion as a Health Coach. The questions that helped me analyze my truest heart desires started with the following: Am I on course with visions I previously set for myself? Am I growing mentally, emotionally, and spiritually? What are the blocks preventing me from living at my maximum potential?

I had to be completely real with myself and see that I truly became complacent, but acknowledged that I needed the break from entrepreneurial efforts. After accepting the awesome full-time role as Health Coach, I literally gave up all thoughts about being an entrepreneur. After working diligently as a full-time entrepreneur for over 2 years, I was burnt out and very discouraged from the constant entrepreneurial efforts needed to maintain momentum. I saw my role as a Health Coach as a dream job and maybe even something I could retire from. It was everything I wanted: a comfortable salary, an opportunity to be a transformational leader, and a great work team. Plus, you can't overlook that I walk to work every day and it only takes me 6 minutes from door-door.

For 10 months, I was just working my 8 hours a day then having the best time of my life. My husband and I spent a ton of money living life like we were on vacation every day. I even created a hashtag on social media: #vacation365. Check out all of the pics on social media!

Then in August 2016, I was sparked to start a 5-day Abundance mindset challenge online. I really don't know what sparked me to join. I think I was intrigued on how I could use this concept to help my patients expand their mindsets to live more abundantly. Little did I know; this engagement would change the trajectory of my personal and business life.

Before the challenge even started I began to research some things regarding the approach and concept associated with the challenge. The leader was using the term "Infinite Receiving". The leader and founder of this concept did videos and posts in her Facebook group. I was really impressed and also felt like it was a place I belong. On the Saturday before the official challenge start date, I decided to chop 9 inches of my hair off symbolizing a fresh start. I really didn't think I would be truly CHANGING my life, but I had an urge to do this and I went for it.

When I returned home that evening I felt like a new woman and was motivated to change the direction of my life. On day 1 of the challenge the coach/leader instructed us to post about what we desire and what we want to infinitely receive. I boldly placed a picture of a woman pregnant with her husband, a house on the lake, and a platform in front of an audience with mic with a very large crowd of people. My life hasn't been the same since this challenge. I went ahead and joined the paid 8 week Masters of Infinite Receiving Experience. Not even a week later, the inspiration hit me to start this book and I was ignited to empower women to claim their unstoppable power for optimum health, infinite prosperity, and fulfillment.

Complacency becomes a comfort zone: a self-assured sense that you are where you need to be and that there is no real room for improvement, nothing more to be discovered or achieved. It could have been easy for me to say, "Oh well, I have my 'comfortable' job as a Health Coach. Why do more?" So many people live with a certain sense of security and comfort with the status quo. Complacency can be a passive contentment, but easily agitated when you scratch the surface. For example, a married couple with the beautiful home who come to resent their overbearing mortgage; the high-powered executive who is overworked and unfulfilled; the parents who love their children but who feel trapped like hamsters in a wheel – I've met all these types of people in my coaching practice. I call them the *"I'm Fine"* squad. These people want more out of life, but it's much easier for them to accept life "as is" instead of doing the work necessary to break free of their own shackles to build a passionate and fulfilling life.

After receiving my awaking message to break the complacency curse, I knew I had to step into my calling to ignite many other beautiful minds. I began truly reflecting on my ideal life and purpose. I began setting up my longterm and short-term goals so that I make sure I walk in my ultimate purpose that I had spoken over my life at Youth Camp when I was 14 years old. Which I will be sharing details of that story in an upcoming chapter.

Time to Slay:

- In what ways, have you been complacent?

- In what ways, have you stretch out of your comfort zone?

- How can you step up your game in every category in your life without feeling overwhelmed?

Chapter 17
Setting Yourself up For Success

> "The key is not to prioritize what's on your schedule, but to schedule your priorities."
> – Stephen Convey

Unstoppable confident women are organized and keep themselves focused with incremental goals. One of the biggest obstacles women face while in pursuit of their happiness in life is making themselves a priority. As women, we wear multiple hats every day with kids, spouses/significant other, work, and business. I have coached many women on how to set boundaries and create balance by focusing on all their priorities starting with putting self-FIRST. Self-care seems to be at the bottom of list or heck not even on a priority list at all. It's imperative you treat yourself as the Queen you are. Remember, you can't pour from an empty cup. All of your tasks each day requires a little bit of volume from your cup. If you don't pamper yourself, eat balanced meals, get dressed up every now or then, or get some type of movement in several times of week then you will start pouring, but nothing will be there to fill the cup of others.

There are three common excuses women say that forces them to avoid making themselves a priority: Not Enough Time, Feeling Guilty, or it Feels Selfish. The more giving and caring a person you are, the more these feelings seem to emerge. What I do recommend is you focus on the impact that your time does have, and give yourself the same attention you'd give someone else you love.

One of my coaching clients struggled so bad to put herself on the top of the to-do list every day at the beginning of our program. She is a full-time working woman, wife and mom of 3 busy kids. When we first started her coaching program, she could barely get a few minutes alone in the restroom, had low self-esteem, and was extremely stressed from the daily extracurricular activities in the evenings with kids. One of her first assignments I gave her in my program was to find 5 mins each day to do something for herself. She started with mirror work in the morning:
sharing with herself 3 things she is proud of with herself, 3 things she forgives herself for, and 1 thing she vowed to do for herself that day.

She did this exercise for 6 out 7 days and when she returned to our coaching call I heard the excitement in her voice on how much better her week was this week vs. the week prior. Take note: nothing changed in her schedule, she didn't lose a miraculous amount of weight that week, the kids weren't away at grandma's, and she didn't win the lottery. All she did was add one simple gesture to her daily agenda which took up to 5mins a day to complete. This gesture helped reprogram her mindset. Instead of being the last on the list each day, she put herself first. Starting her day off with mirror work completely flipped the priorities and energetic feeling of her actions.

Now she was the first person she spoke to in the morning and got the attention and love needed to fuel her day. As she continued in my program she began to feel amazing in her skin to the point she was able to walk across the floor at her place of work with confidence and grace. She didn't need to lose weight to feel great in her skin. Then a week later out of nowhere her husband bought her flowers with a special card. She shared with me that he never does things like this and it was such perfect timing since they were struggling with their connection lately. All of these awesome shifts started with her placing herself at the top of the to-do list each day.

Please do not feel guilty about allocating personal time for yourself. It's nothing more than taking some time to put aside from your everyday business and treating yourself to an activity that you enjoy. Do what my client did, allocate 5mins at the beginning of the day to do something for you; it gives you an opportunity to Relax, Refocus and Recharge. And when you do that, you can come back to your responsibilities with greater focus, commitment and enjoyment.

Time to Slay:

How can you adopt more self-care habits in your day to-day? Think about what are the potential barriers preventing you from investing in self. Then create an action plan to change those habits within the next 30days. It only takes 21 days to make or break habits! Make taking care of self as simple and habitual as brushing your teeth on a daily basis. Do you notice you don't have to say, 'I need to squeeze in teeth brushing time in my schedule" or "When will I be able to brush my teeth again"? It just happens every single day. The same thing will happen with your self-care routine.

Keep shifting the mindset and keep the momentum going.

Here are some ways to start setting up boundaries to make yourself a priority:

1. Before you start booking your calendar with agendas, extracurricular activities with the kids, or projects, put in calendar ONE DAY a week which you do something nice for yourself. It can be taking a 30min bath, reading a book, playing a game, handing out with friends or etc.

2. Don't do everything for your children (unless they are an infant). They are able to do some tasks on their own. Take the time to teach them how to do things for themselves.

3. Learn the art of saying NO, the ability to delegate and the capacity to accept help without feeling guilty. Remember that no matter what we do, there are only 24 hours in a day and 168hrs/wk., so you can't create more time. But you can clear some time by reevaluating priorities, perhaps saying "NO" more often and practicing smart time management.

Chapter 18
Fresh Start

> "Nobody can go back and start a new beginning, but anyone can start today and make a new ending." – Maria Robinson

I knew from the time that I was a young teenager that I was called to a higher purpose. I just never knew what my distinct purpose to follow or the ideal life I desired to experience. Church of God 1999 Youth Camp is where I became aware of my calling to be a leader, but still lacked details on what that meant for my life.

Youth camp as always was a 4-day outing packed with so much fun and life-changing encounters. Our church bus arrived to the site before 12pm on day one and it was roughly 200 teenagers on the camp ground in the southern part of Ohio towards the end of June. It was exciting to meet so many fellow teens from other Church of God denominations within the Ohio Region. This was my first-time attending Youth Camp so I stuck close to my clique from my youth group including my friend, Sulai. We started our mornings with a sing-off, the one song that reminds me of Youth Camp was sang by a veteran Youth Camp Leader (19 years later, he still attends camp) singing, "Ain't no rock gonna cry in my place". When I hear this song, it brings back so many happy moments.

Throughout the day our Youth Camp leaders led us in many water sport activities and other games. I am not sure if our Youth Pastor was having more fun than us; he was goofy and a big kid. He would come around teasing us and squirting us with water guns. We played so many games during the daytime. After hours of play and socializing, it was time to get ready for 7pm evening services outside in the tent. One evening, as I was getting ready, my palms were getting sweaty and I couldn't find a comfortable outfit to wear that evening to save my life. I think I went through 3-4 full outfits before selecting the final one. Then I looked into the mirror and had an enormous god-awful zit on my left nostril. It looked like those bumps you watch on a viral YouTube video that will have a very nasty explosion. I was embarrassed and all of a sudden I didn't want to go to service. Sulai and another friend kept encouraging me and we even tried to use their makeup to cover it up. I was happy that the makeup at least minimized the white head and shine from the bump.

When we walked into the tent, I could truly feel a different energy. An over-whelming calm presence as the worship team sang their songs and the musicians (drummer, bass player, and pianist) followed their flow. It didn't take me long to start clapping and allow the prior frustrations to melt away. As I was leaning into the worship music, I became emotional and thanked God for his blessings. The tent was filled with worshipping teenagers. The preacher/speaker for that evening didn't even get to his agenda. The music kept playing one song after another. You could hear some teens weeping and shouting. 80% of hands were raised and everyone was singing in unison.

Our speaker went to the platform where the podium was placed and started calling teens out to come to the alter to pray over them. I was one of those teenagers and I felt overwhelmed in the presence and really didn't have time to think about or rationalize what was going to happen. I instantly walked to the alter. The speaker had the musicians silence their music. He looked me in my eyes and explained to me that God told him to share with me this message, "You are a special gift, everything you have been through and will go through will be used to uplift others, and you are a leader for many." I cried so hard and could feel the hands of God wrap me with love. Of course, I really didn't know what that message all meant at that present time. However, I felt the power cover me love and peace.

The last bit of that chip on my shoulder was removed as I cast my cares and concerns over to Jesus. At that moment, the void of my heart was filled with God's love and I began to start speaking in tongues and jumping. I will never forget those words and this experience. I felt the power of God and it changed the trajectory of my life.

I returned home in so much awe of what happened over the course of those 4 days. My life has honestly never been the same since that encounter. What will it take for you to change the direction of your life? Have you had a similar experience which provided a fresh start?

Sometimes it can be a deeply spiritual moment and sometimes it can appear as a simple choice. Similar to how I chopped off 9 inches of my hair prior to that Infinite Receiving Facebook challenge. It was a simple decision, but to me it was a bold declaration that I was starting fresh. Besides feeling a tad bit sassier, the change attracted enormous number of blessings and provided so much more clarity on my journey. It's crazy how that happens; I truly felt like I made room to receive more clarity and blessings into my life.

Sometimes the feeling of "starting over" can be daunting. When I announced that I was completely revamping my online coaching services, I instantly felt overwhelmed thinking starting from scratch was a negative task added to my life. I went from a Weight Management Coach to a Tenacity and Empowerment Coach for women. I started a new Facebook group and began new marketing strategies. At moments, I became frustrated thinking, "Wow, I am starting all over again." I needed a new email list, new followers, and new strategy. It can be overwhelming; however, it is also very exciting to take a plunge into something new and refreshing. I had to get control of my thoughts and reframe my circumstances by asking myself, "What's the worst that can happen? If I hate it, at least I gave it a try!" It all ended up working out very well and I began to acquire clients for my new business venture.

I am here to give you hope and encouragement that it's ok to feel like you may be starting over and it is ok if it is uncomfortable thinking about life and goals in a new way.
Either situation, I want you to proclaim a fresh new start. This is your wake-up, Queen!

It's time to slay! Declare a fresh start:
   -A new pattern of thoughts
   -A new wave of emotions.
   -A new connection to the world
   -A new belief system in yourself
   -A new source of tenacity

Time to Slay:

- What can you do to symbolize a fresh start in your life?
- How will accomplishing this goal change your life?
- What will you do differently this time around?
- Could this possibly expand your confidence? Environment? Income?

Chapter 19

Snap your Rubber band Snap
(Move Beyond Own Limits)

> "Expanding capacity requires a willingness to endure short-term discomfort in the service of long-term reward."- Jim Loehr and Tony Schwartz, *The Power of Full Engagement*

School for me was very rough. I struggled with comprehension. I hated reading books and couldn't write a decent paragraph to save my life. I barely survived middle school. High school I started to try to shift gears, but my first year of college I felt so dumb. I couldn't keep up, failed several tests, and couldn't get my thoughts on paper appropriately. One of my professors wrote on an assignment, "This is middle school material." Ouch! Since then I've struggled with placing judgment on myself regarding my writing abilities. I really didn't know what I was going to do so I took the easy way out; I dropped out of college and jumped on a greyhound bus to Texas to marry the love of my life. Crazy right!?! (it's more to "greyhound" story in an upcoming chapter.)

No one wants to get snapped by a rubber band, it hurts! When a rubber band returns to its original size, I call that shrinking. Probably 80% of the time we don't even stretch the rubber band as far as it truly can go because we are afraid of the consequences of it snapping our eyes. How have you done this with your dreams and aspirations? You get an awesome thought to start a business (the rubber band starts expanding) then you start questioning how much money you will need to invest in self or business tools to get started (shrinking). Another example, you start stepping into your passion to be a public speaker (expanding) then you begin to think about your aesthetics and start comparing yourself to others (shrinking). In order to keep expanding you have to stay tenacious on moving past every obstacle and mindset block. The object is to keep expanding your rubber band a little more and more and more each day.

When you keep pressing forward you continuously expand the rubber band. Don't be afraid of the band snapping because all that means is its time to upgrade to a larger and more advance version. When you are expanding in life you stretch like a rubber band. Do you know that feeling when you have the rubber band and it's about to snap because its stretch so far out and all the fear within begins to rise thinking it's going to snap if we go too far? Scary, right? But that is precisely what you must do. Stretch to snapping and then grab a bigger brand to stretch.

Time to Slay:

- How can you expand more in life?

- What can you do to stretch yourself out of your comfort zone? What will be the worst that can happen if your rubber band snaps? Remember the snapping of the rubber band is a GREAT thing. You must get comfortable being uncomfortable!

- Have you ever had to dig beyond deep within self to find the strength to make something happen? Well good job on being tenacious with those efforts! If not, how can you dig deeper with your goals?

Chapter 20
Rewrite your Story

> **Edit your life frequently and ruthlessly. It's your masterpiece after all." – Nathan W. Morris**

Writing this book is HUGE for me. I feel like I've upgraded from a rubber band to a heavy-duty resistance workout band. Many times, through the process I questioned my ability to write and create a clear and concise manuscript. I was even super scared to have my editor read it because, I was afraid of being judged for my writing abilities. I started shrinking by associating my past of what that professor said to me during my first year of college. Even to this day, I struggle with feeling dumb, I get limiting thoughts about my ability to be a creative writer because of old test scores and past struggles I had in school. Remember when I dropped out of college? Well I continued the journey some years later.

My husband had joined the United States Air Force, 4 months after we got engaged in 2002. We were planning a wedding for March 2003 in Cleveland, OH. He was held back in technical training school which forced us to move the wedding date. Between the frustrations of college and his military shenanigans, I made a bold & tenacious move (nothing new) to go get my man via a greyhound bus! After we got married in Wichita Falls, TX courthouse we were stationed in Seattle, WA (first duty station), I worked in banking and still had this desire to go to school, but couldn't figure out how to integrate this in my schedule while working full-time. 4 years later, I decided to return to school, I was ready to try this again with a different mindset.

I started with University of Phoenix (UOP) and had classes on campus once a week. I loved the collaboration approach UOP had with working as a team for papers and projects. I began to cultivate my strengths; my team mates discovered that I was a great public speaker and would accept the task to present our research to the class without hesitation. I also learned during my time with UOP that I was good at organizing data, but still struggled with translating it in a concise manner. This was a turning point for me, the team approach with this school allowed me to lean on the rest of my teammates while I strengthened my weaknesses. As I began to build self- efficacy in my skill sets, I began to build a more "unstoppable" mindset.

Five years later I finished my education at Cleveland State University (we moved from WA to OH) graduated Magna Cum Laude with my Bachelor's degree. You would never think this same girl who struggled so much and had no confidence to obtain a degree could pull something like this off. I remember getting my first "A" paper on MY OWN (without a team, similar to UOP classrooms) at Cleveland State University. It was a 20-page paper requiring a lot of details and research. I blasted through that assignment and was only a few points away from a perfect score. I was beyond proud, because I knew how far I had come on this journey. Sometimes it takes a little support to obtain our goals.

We need people in our lives as we ride around in our journey to be the rear and side view mirrors. We need people to cover our blinds spots until we get clearer on our vision. We sometimes need people validating our gifts and celebrating our success to propel us to the next level. In 2013, I finished my Master's Degree and now I am currently enrolled in a Doctoral Program.

Remember you can rewrite your story at any time. Maybe your family members don't value education, or maybe you don't feel like you are smart enough or have enough money to obtain your degree. If there is a will there is ALWAYS a way. Whatever your dream is, you have to believe it can happen and it will happen. Don't worry about the how, just take a moment and think about this goal you want to accomplish that has been lingering over your head for a while.

Time to Slay:

- What story do you most often hear yourself telling?
- What story is holding you back?
- What would you try now if you knew you could not fail?
- How can you begin to start rewriting your story?

Chapter 21
Setting Goals (Long & Short-term)

> "You significantly enhance your chances of completing a goal if you actually get started. Breaking down your tasks into bite-sized, palatable, digestible pieces are what will actually help you get started." – Lisa Nichols

What you want to avoid in your quest in the envisioning of your life, is dreaming so far past your reality – or the current circumstances - that you end up abandoning your goals and damaging your self-esteem. In order to avoid this soul-sucking episode, reframe from wishful thinking. It's ok to envision your ideal life and attach an emotional component to your vision, but it's imperative to set believable and achievable goals for every segment of life you are in. Up until now I have encouraged you to dream without considering the "strategy". Now I feel like you are ready to go the next level.

> "I am living a purposeful life. My actions align with my dreams."
> -Unknown

Goals are needed to succeed because it provides focus. Goal setting not only allows you to take control of your life's direction; it also provides you a benchmark for determining whether you are actually succeeding. Think about it: having a million dollars in the bank is only proof of success if one of your goals is to amass riches. If your goal is to practice acts of charity, then keeping the money for yourself is suddenly contrary to how you would define success.

To accomplish your goals, however, you need to know how to set them. You can't simply say, "I want" and expect it to happen. Goal setting is a process that starts with careful consideration of what you want to achieve, and ends with a lot of hard work to actually do it. In between there are some very well defined steps that transcend the specifics of each goal. Knowing these steps will allow you to formulate goals that you can accomplish.
Here are our five golden rules of goal setting:

Set Goals that Excite You
When you set goals for yourself, it is important that they motivate you; this means making sure that they are important to you, and that there is value in achieving them. If you have little interest in the outcome, or they are irrelevant given the larger picture, then the chances of you putting in the work to make them happen are slim.
Motivation is key to achieving goals.

Set goals that relate to the high priorities in your life. Without this type of focus, you can end up with far too many goals, leaving you too little time to devote to each one. Goal achievement requires commitment, so to maximize the likelihood of success, you need to feel a sense of urgency and have an "I must do this" attitude. When you don't have this, you risk putting off what you need to do to make the goal a reality. This in turn leaves you feeling disappointed and frustrated with yourself, both of which are de-motivating. And you can end up in a very destructive "I can't do anything or be successful at anything" frame of mind.

Tip:
To make sure your goal is exciting, write down why it's valuable and important to you. Ask yourself, "If I were to share my goal with others, what would I tell them to convince them it was a worthwhile goal?" You can use this motivating value statement to help you if you start to doubt yourself or lose confidence in your ability to actually make the goal happen.

Create S.M.A.R.T Goals
You have probably heard of S.M.A.R.T goals already. But do you always apply the rule? The simple fact is that for goals to be powerful, they should be designed to be SMART. There are many variations of what SMART stands for, but the essence is this – goals should be:

- Specific.
- Measurable.
- Attainable.
- Relevant.
- Time Bound.

Set Specific Goals
Your goal must be clear and well defined. Vague or generalized goals are unhelpful because they don't provide sufficient direction. Remember, you need goals to show you the way. Make it as easy as you can to get where you want to go by defining precisely where you want to end up.

Set Measurable Goals
Include precise amounts, dates, and so on in your goals so you can measure your degree of success. If your goal is

simply defined as "increase income" how will you know when you have been successful? In one month's time if you have a 1 percent increase or in two years' time when you have a 10 percent increase? Without a way to measure your success you miss out on the celebration that comes with knowing you have actually achieved something.

Set Attainable Goals
Make sure that it's possible to achieve the goals you set. If you set a goal that you have no hope of achieving, you will only demoralize yourself and erode your confidence.

However, resist the urge to set goals that are too easy. Accomplishing a goal that you didn't have to work hard for can be anticlimactic at best, and can also make you fear setting future goals that carry a risk of non-achievement. By setting realistic yet challenging goals, you hit the balance you need. These are the types of goals that require you to "raise the bar" and they bring the greatest personal satisfaction.

Set Relevant Goals
Goals should be relevant to the direction you want your life to take. By keeping goals aligned with this, you'll develop the focus you need to get ahead and do what you want. Set widely scattered and inconsistent goals, and you'll go in circles wasting your time – and your life – away.

Set Time-Bound Goals

Your goals must have a deadline. Again, this means that you know when you can celebrate success. When you are working on a deadline, your sense of urgency increases and achievement will come that much quicker.

Put Goals in Writing
The physical act of writing down a goal makes it real and tangible. When your goal is written down there are no excuses about forgetting about them. As you write, use the word "will" instead of "would like to" or "might." For example, "I will become Best Selling Author" not "I would like to become Best Selling Author." The first goal statement has power and you can "see" yourself becoming the best-selling author, the second lacks passion and very passive in its efforts which will give room to provide excuses if the goal is not achieved.

> *Tip*:
> Post your goals in visible places to remind yourself every day of what it is you intend to do. Put them on your walls, phone wallpaper, desk, computer monitor, bathroom mirror or refrigerator as a constant reminder.

Take Action
Similar to our discussion regarding visualization, you can't just write the goals down and pray that they will come to manifestation through osmosis. Even though I am a true believer in miraculous healing, I also believe dreams are goals with deadlines. Dreaming alone will not cut it. Yes, this is the time to consider the "how" of the plan, but not get too focused on it. Action is often missed in the process

of goal setting. It's easy to become focused on the outcome and then the plan of all the steps to get to intentions are forgotten along the way. By having a list of intentions with steps then crossing each one off the list will provide a sense of pride and accomplishment. This is especially important if your goal is a big stretch and demanding, or long-term.

Be Consistent
Remember, goal setting is an ongoing activity not just a means to an end. Build in reminders to keep yourself on track, and make regular time-slots available to review your goals. Your end destination may remain quite similar over the long term, but the action plan you set for yourself along the way can change significantly. Make sure the relevance, value, and necessity remain high. *"Success is the sum of small efforts. Repeated day in and day out."* – Unknown

Time to Slay:

- Are your personal standards high enough to reach your goals?
- How can you change the world for generations to come?
- What plan do you need in order to achieve your dreams? What are you willing to commit to? Who/What do you need as a resource to ensure you execute goals?
- Is this the best outcome you can create or is there something greater?

SECTION 3:
OVERCOME OBSTACLES

Chapter 22
It's Time to Slay

> **"When God sees you doing your part, developing what he has given you, then He will do his part and open doors that no man can shut." -Unknown**

"Independent" and "Assertive" would be the two words to describe me as a child. When I wanted something, I got it, when I had something to say, I said it. My mom and sister are a bit different: they are quiet and reserved. They never make themselves known in a room full of people and hesitate to speak up when needed. They are intimidated by crowds and consistently take the safe zone. NOT ME! That has never been me, I am the exact opposite. I don't even think I know what a "safe route" is. There is "no chill" to my efforts. If I could go 200% effort, I would and make tenacious choices each and every day.

I naturally stand out in a crowd of people. You will hear my voice in the distance, I will be making a joke, sharing my experience, or asking questions. I am a TRUE extrovert. Introverts: don't you go thinking you can't be tenacious as well. You too can adopt the "unstoppable" persona to your character. Even though I am an extrovert, my tenacious spirit is an inner effort firmly grasping my desires every step on my path.

Tenacity doesn't mean just external hard-work; it requires a lot of inner work and soul searching. It's taking a deep dive within yourself to continually remove mindset blocks, heal the conditions of the heart, and embrace the feelings of being uncomfortable at times.

I have cultivated this tenacious character of mine year after year. Healing one heartache after another and slaying one mindset block after another block. Every level I expanded myself to give me another version of a "rubber band". Every new expansion required a new mindset, new environment, and new resources. The majority of the time when I expanded, self-doubt and a surge of negative emotions would rise to the surface. Once the emotions arose I would be left with the thoughts of lack, setbacks, and failures. This is when true power of tenacity kicks in.

As we discussed in section 1, you know what these thoughts can lead to. Within section 3 of this book, I want you to look at all your dreams and desires as "strategies" and think about how you can creatively overcome potential obstacles to stay 5-10 steps ahead of the game. To achieve any goal, you have to take a moment and create "if--then" solutions for every problem you foresee on your path. I know you are not telepathic, but it's imperative to create a plan B, C, D, E, or even F case scenarios to ensure you leave opportunity for ZERO excuses. When you develop a no matter what plan with a "can do" attitude you are setting yourself up for success to effectively achieve every dream you wrote down on your 500-dream sheet.

When I took a mini survey of people's thoughts about the word "tenacity", the word stubbornness came up a few times. At first thought it could work—except the word stubborn brings about a negative trait and on the other side there is strength in stubbornness. A few other words came up in the survey: perseverance, persistence, stamina, power, and strength.

Webster defines Tenacity as: "the quality or fact of being very determined; determination the quality or fact of continuing to exist; persistence".

My definition of tenacity is *unflinching faith and relentless action derived from continuous improvement of your inner self.*

As you can see I put a slightly different twist on the concept of tenacity. The definition is derived from my countless encounters of slaying goals throughout my entire life. Yes, external work is required, but I have learned the core of tenacity evolves from within.

The Mighty Caterpillar by Rev. Linda MartellaWhitsett

One morning on retreat, while silently sipping coffee outdoors, I listened to life going on around me. The Cibolo Creek was babbling. A red bird called from a nearby tree, two high-pitched whistles followed by seven chirps, over and over again. Shrubbery rustled in a light breeze. The day had begun.

Swiping at my leg in response to feeling something on it, I saw the "something" was not a dried oak leaf like the ones that were raining all over me. I swiped at a small caterpillar-*like critter. It landed on the deck next to my chair. Being in a state of quiet awareness, I watched the insect place some feet in along. It moved, undaunted, over the gaps between deck slats. It found the leg of my chair and began climbing.*

When it reached the top, it projected more than half its mass over the edge of the chair, feeling for its next support and *finding it on the surface of the table close by. It kept going until it could not sense a surface on which to proceed, at which time it doubled back, curled its long body around, arcing like a divining rod until it found solid land. All the other feet followed.*

The busy little creature travelled a great distance, by caterpillar standards. It never seemed to be concerned with whether it was upright or sideways, retracing its steps or in new territory. Every time it came to an abyss, it paused long enough to feel its way to the next solid ground.

I was thinking, as I observed the creature teacher, that I would do well to feel my way forward by the power of tenacity. Persisting non-anxiously is the activity of tenacity. Tenacity, along with stability and courage, makes up the habits of spiritual strength".

Every queen must face her battles. The key is to prepare for them and be unstoppable as you charge through them with ease and grace. It might be scary and uncomfortable, but your throne is worth it. Do you have goals and dreams that seem incredibly out of reach? Or, maybe you feel like you need to put work, family and other responsibilities first—so your personal goals get pushed off. You are not alone! Remember, your power is based in the tenacity of your heart. Draw forth tenacity from within during unsteady circumstances so that you do not give up prematurely and remain committed to the cause as you actively seek the level of your path.

No more playing small…remember you are a Queen! It's time to slay! As you proceed on this unique journey, your visions will become much clearer on every step of the way. You have to uncover your tenacity and embrace the tigress within; God has provided all infinite resources for you to achieve the life of your dreams. It's up to you to step into the mindset of having unstoppable tenacity. Are you ready to slay?

Time to Slay:

- What is the definition of tenacity for you? How is it defined in your life?

- How can you get the eye of the tiger in life to become unstoppable?

- How bad do you really want to achieve those 500 dreams listed out? What will it take for you go all in and put all of your energy into achieving the life that you have always dreamed of?

- Thinking about your current hopes and dreams, what role could courage play? If you were courageous, what might you do?

- Identify a situation in your present experience that calls for the light of strength. What thoughts and acts could demonstrate stability, courage, and tenacity?

- Create or select a symbol for strength to display where you will see it often. Here are some examples: an image, an original drawing, collage, or sculpture. You can wear it, place the image on your desktop or wallpaper of your phone.

Chapter 23
Take Control of your Life

> "One morning she woke up different. Done with trying to figure out who was with her, against her, or walking down the middle because they didn't have the guts to pick a side. She was done with anything that didn't bring peace. She realized that opinions were a dime a dozen, validation was for parking, and loyalty wasn't a word, but a lifestyle. It was this day that her life changed. And not because of a man, or a job, but because she realized that life is way too short to leave *the* key to your happiness in someone else's pocket." - Unknown

I was a steady 150 pounds for most of my adult life until, thanks to a bizarre twist of fate (a terrible ankle injury that resulted in 5 screws and 1 plate), my weight skyrocketed and I gained an additional 25 pounds due to the lack of movement and increased food consumption. While that might not sound like a lot, at only 5'2", I definitely felt and noticed the additional pounds. Seeing that number on the scale at a doctor's appointment was absolutely terrifying. I felt sluggish, insecure, and lost on where to start to make a change.

I made a decision to take control of my life. I was feeling frustrated, worn out and tired of the circles; enough was enough! I was tired of making career aspirations #1 priority, tired of saying "I'll start tomorrow" and was done with the excuses! I knew it was time for me to make myself a priority and that's when I saw the one thing that would really drive my weight loss journey. The pink bikini! There I was, flipping through Prevention Magazine when I came across an adorable pink swimsuit that I knew I had to have. This little number was so dang cute and I became obsessed with fitting into it. I knew, deep in my heart, that one day I would wear that thing and that was the moment I declared my intention to ditch the extra pounds and get serious about my health. Don't get me wrong, I had my fair share of haters who shot me the side eye, but I was determined.

I kept my routine simple at first. I started eating right and working out like a mad woman, but the shift really came not just because of those things, but because I was finally putting myself first. What really changed for me was the intention to care for myself first and to love the body I already had. Of course, there were tons of obstacles and frustrations and at times I almost wanted to give up. The first few months on my journey I gained 8lbs. I didn't know at that time weight training and my new fitness routines were causing my body to retain water. But then I would remember my pink bikini and all the emotions imagining myself wearing it on a beach over took the frustration and turned it into pure excitement. I honestly didn't have a clue on "how" I was going to achieve this goal; I just knew and felt in my heart it would be achieved one day.

Twenty-two months later, I lost a total of 65lbs and I was ready to wear my pink bikini. The whole journey I drooled over a picture of the pink bikini I ripped out of the Prevention magazine and never bought it until I felt ready. My husband and I had a trip planned to go to Puerto Rico in

Oct 2012 and I knew this would be a perfect moment to head over to a large-chain lingerie store at the mall to purchase my very own pink bikini. I was beaming with excitement and felt like I was in a dream. I had the largest smile possible on my face. The store clerk passed me my bikini and my heart started pumping and emotion began to flood my mind. I instantly thought back when I stepped on the scale at the doctor's visit and just knew I needed to make a change in my life. I looked in the mirror and said with heavy emotion, "You did it, Erica!" Then I eagerly began to change into it and instantly felt so amazing in the bikini. I was very pleased with the work and effort I put into my health for the last couple of years. When I arrived home, I walked around at home with the bikini on a few times prior to strutting my stuff at the beach. You honestly couldn't tell me anything because I knew what it took to be on this side of the fence.

I didn't stop there; I was able walk the stage twice as a Bikini Fitness Competitor. I had the desire in Jan 2014 to do step on stage, but had doubts/fear (like any normal person). When my husband left for deployment in April 2014, I made a more concrete decision to pursue this goal. It was super fun at first: the muscle gain, tighter body, additional knowledge in nutrition BUT things got real in the final 4 weeks.

I had several financial issues to pay for all of the expenses (this show cost me well over $2600). Now this may not be a lot of money to some of you, but we were living off one income at this time and my start-up business. Also, the hard work while on low carbs was NO joke! I was taking 3 hour naps and STILL going to sleep at 10pm. I really can't see how people do these shows while working 9-5 jobs, being parents, or even having their spouses home, but I know several people who do it. I salute them!

The final week for me was super emotional/stressful since I was so scared I was losing muscle mass, my body wasn't doing what I wanted it to do. I was water depleting and feeling like my muscles were flat. I started to doubt I could even do this. I questioned the whole process 4 days out! I thought being this close I should be having fun with all the pampering, but then I got menstrual cramps and felt like, I almost died! I don't know about you ladies, but I gain 35lbs of water weight EVERY month around that time and it sits on my stomach. I was like, "really? All this hard work to be bloated on stage in a bikini in front of hundreds of people!" I was super upset. To top it off, I got a notification that my PayPal account had fraudulent charges that took my funds to cover final expenses for the show. Then I had family drama I had to deal with which was not the perfect timing since I was already stressing!

Finally, on 2 days out I actually told myself, "girl you need to pray"! Then it's like the Lord began to give me a new mind and creative ideas on how to solve my dilemmas. I took Gas-X, Midol, and Dandelion Root capsules to dry up the bloat, out of nowhere unexpected funds dropped into my account, and family dispute was resolved. It all worked out! When I walked the stage I was truly proud of myself for pressing through with tenacity. I didn't even really care about winning a trophy; I felt like I already won by tenaciously pressing forward. I ended up winning 2nd place in my class for my first bikini fitness competition. I then went on and walked the stage 3 weeks later to win two more trophies in 2nd place.

As you can see my also known name, Queen of Tenacity, is true to my lifestyle, I have recognized that everything I have been through has created me to be this tenacious powerhouse woman. I am honored to help you dig within yourself and find your tenacious creature. Tenacity is not about luck, it's a way of thinking. Each day on my journey I am silencing gremlins in my mind attempting to stop me from achieving my dreams.

Taking control of your life requires effort and consistent behaviors. The advice I have for others struggling with weight loss is to not focus so much on the number on the scale. I ended up losing the weight in 22 months but what I gained was even more fabulous. A trust, confidence and love for myself I never even thought was possible. And see, that's the thing. People think "losing weight" is the answer to happiness, and that quick fixes and deprivation diets and crazy "probably not FDA approved pills" will do the work for them. But if you really want to be healthy and get all the good stuff that comes along with it (confidence, thriving relationships, a successful business, and etc.), you really just have to choose yourself first!

Did you know that 85% of women do not like playing dress up because they do not like how they look or feel? Why is this?

From personal experience and working with clients, women who are dealing with esteem issues use "weight loss goals" as their scapegoat since its tangible and seems more controllable, but most of the time these women are dealing with deeply ingrained emotional pain such as:

- Unworthiness
- Not Enough Syndrome
- Perfectionism (All or Nothing mindset)
- Lack of Purpose/Passion

As you progress on your journey, take it one day at a time and embrace yourself while you are in the "in-between" stage of your journey. If you don't like yourself or how you look in the mirror, your brain goes crazy with scarcity thoughts like, "I'm not good enough." Since our brain doesn't know the difference between a thought and the truth, over time you start to believe the language you are speaking to yourself. One of the best ways to start reprogramming your mindset to help on a weight loss journey is to speak life over your body through morning mantras to energetically release stubborn weight? The same energy and focus you place in your life and business to be successful, serve your clients, and increase prosperity applies to your body as well. In addition, it's critical to celebrate all of your victories (scale and non-scale) along the way.

Time to Slay:

- How can you take control over your life? In what area, will you focus on?
- Create your own Health & Wellness Mantra List: Every morning when you get up, DO NOT check emails, FB newsfeed, or anything else. I want you

to wake up and recite your gratitude list then start speaking these mantras over your life:
- ✓ I am learning how to love my body
- ✓ Trusting my body is becoming easier and easier
- ✓ Healing is happening in my body and in my mind
- ✓ I am feeling healthier and stronger with each day that passes
- ✓ Everything I eat heals me and nourishes me
- ✓ Making small changes is becoming easier for me
- ✓ I am choosing progress over perfection
- ✓ I am feeling healthy, focused and determined
- ✓ You'll be surprised the power/strength received to transform your body through daily weight loss mantras! Remember when you feel good you attract good things.

Chapter 24

The Power of Tenacity

> "There are some things in life that may come easy, but most things worth having or achieving will only come with dedication and tenacity."
> -Germaine Moody

The start of a new semester towards my bachelor's degree had me on cloud on 9. That morning I put on my most favorite jeans (you know the ones which make you feel like a true queen with the perfect curves?) and I even put some extra time in doing my hair and makeup. I was so ready to get this semester started. Being back in school at this time was still a bit new for me. I still had another couple of years to go to complete my degree, but I was really trying to embrace the journey and just have fun studying as I pursued my bachelor's degree. At this time of our marriage we were living with my mom, step-father, sister, and brother due to financial constraints and goals. The weather outside that January in Ohio was cold, but no snow. We had black ice that day. I really didn't know, since it looked rainy outside. I grabbed my book bag which had a very heavy Art History book and Earth Science book within. I proceeded outside since my husband was going to drop me off on campus and right at the moment he was locking the door behind me I slipped on a black icy stair. My right foot flew into the air while the book shifted to my left side of body which placed an enormous amount of pressure on my left ankle and I fell on the ground into a pretzel position. I couldn't get up and didn't feel any pain until my husband rushed to grab me from the bottom of the 3-stair case porch. When he picked me up, all I felt was this weird dangling feeling on my left foot.

When he got me in the house all the pain shot right up from my left ankle to my back and I felt this throbbing pain. My autistic baby brother at that time was about 5 years old and he started obnoxiously laughing, my mom came into the living room and started asking a trillion questions. All I could do is tell everybody to "shut up" I actually cursed because it was too much going on, but no one tending to this ankle of mine. I kept saying with tears, "I think I broke it!" Joshua tried to pick me up and I refused to be touched again because the pain was out this world. My mom called for an ambulance to come to pick me up. I was still fully clothed with a hat, gloves, and coat on from the planned trip to get dropped off at school. As I waited, I felt my heart beating so fast in synch with the throbbing pain in my foot and sweat dripping from my face. I wouldn't be shocked if I was discolored at that moment, maybe in flush red or white due to excruciating pain.

When the ambulance arrived, I was still in severe pain and was giving technicians such a hard time because my foot was twisted in my boot and everyone wanted to remove the boot. After fighting with everyone and arguing about the boot somehow it got removed and it was NOT a pretty sight to see. My foot was super swollen and mangled, but we were unsure of the condition.

The ride to hospital was horrible. I really believe they were paying me back for all my attitude I gave at the house about removing the boot (when I am in pain, I am MEAN). They rode over every pot hole in the city of Cleveland they could find. The pain was just indescribable. Just think, my foot was basically dangling so every bump rattled the foot hurt more and more for approximately 20 long mins. I believed I cringed and cried the whole ride there. I arrived at the hospital, and all I can remember was me fighting (again) with staff but this time about my favorite jeans, they couldn't slide them off of me because how damaged my foot was due to the ankle injury. They ended up having to cut the most perfect jeans off of me. Those jeans to this day were the best jeans I ever had as an adult. I think I actually started crying just for the jeans at that point (it was that serious). After the x-ray, they discovered how bad the break was and needed to do surgery, but due to all of the swelling I had to return home and wait.

For 48 hours, I laid around with a very swollen and distorted ankle taking a high dose of medications at my inlaws' house. I was completely zoned out of it and slept most of the time. After the 48 hours passed, we met my Orthopedic Surgeon for the first time. He came into the room very calm, cool, and collected. He begins to start small talk with us, asking how we were doing, jokes about the crazy weather, and conversations about so many people broke bones in the last week due to black ice while softly touching my ankle to examine it and then out of nowhere he aggressively snapped my ankle in place.

My husband said my shoulders were planted on the bed while the surgeon gripped my ankle and my butt lifted straight in the air with a loud scream. At least the pain with the surgeon was quick and straight to the point. Seriously, he caught me completely off guard, I could have killed him. I get the point of making sure I don't tense up to relocate ankle, but wow! He shocked me! I am not sure if the ride in the ambulance or that pain was worse. BOTH were horrible for me!

After I got my composure, my surgeon began to share with me more details on how I broke my ankle. I severely broke my fibular and tibia, I also dislocated the tibia which damaged my peroneus longus tendon. The only thing that didn't get affected was my Achilles tendon. He said, "You will have to get surgery to repair the damage with approximately 1 plate and 6-8 screws" and he further explained how my life could be affected from this injury (as I mentioned in the previous chapter). However, because of all the swelling I wasn't able to get surgery for almost 3 weeks. I was placed in a cast to start the healing process and they set my date for surgery at the end of Feb. I was very scared and nervous about the surgery and how it would affect me, but somehow I managed to shift my thoughts and decided to just go with the flow.

I began to focus on my school work. I was frustrated that I didn't even get a chance to start Spring Semester and was truly concerned about finishing my classes. I immediately contacted all 4 of my professors via email to explain to them my current circumstance and that I would not be able to attend classes on campus that semester. Two professors explained to me that they could not accommodate my request and encouraged me to drop their classes for that semester. My Art History and Earth Science professors both agreed to work with me. They both created an agenda for me to follow so that I was a part of the class and could turn my assignments in along with the other class mates. I was so beyond thankful to be able to continue my goal in obtaining a bachelor's degree.

I was on OxyContin, Vicodin, and Tylenol Codeine for months even while in school. There were many days I was completely spaced out. I couldn't even form a sentence to have a conversation with anyone. All I would do is stare at the ceiling and be in "la-la" land. Somehow I was still getting assignments done, to this day I can't recall doing homework for about 2 weeks. After my surgery, I decided to wean myself off these medications because I felt very high and spacy every day. I didn't feel like myself. The OxyContin is sold as a drug to addicts and I knew I had to stop taking before I suffered long-term consequences. I did suffer a few withdrawal symptoms: fever, headaches, more pain of course from my ankle, and increased food cravings. I started to feel extremely depressed; infertility sorrows began to rise back to the surface and felt insignificant because my mom and hubby had to help me get to the bathroom, shower, and feed me every day for approximately 4 months. I cried so many days during this time frame and was gaining weight by the day. This was the worst-case scenario to put an independent Type A personality trait individual with control issues in.

Somehow I managed to stay on top of my school assignments and was focused to pass both classes. I didn't enjoy the courses as I wanted to, but I did finish BOTH classes with a "B" and with all that was going on, I was extremely proud of myself.

I further impressed myself as I began physical therapy earlier than my Orthopedic Surgeon wanted me to begin. I was tired of being on my back all day and wanted to get mobile as soon as I could. I went into physical therapy (PT) 6 weeks earlier than recommended. My physical therapist was so proud of me. I went in 3 times a week and did routines at home. The hardest routine I had to do during those sessions was pick up triangles from the floor while keeping the injured foot planted on floor. Activating my calves, hamstring, and dorsiflexion in left ankle was challenging.

As I bent down to grab cones it feels like my ankle was a block of steel. There were many times I would allow myself to fall to avoid flexing the ankle. My ankle would be sore days after physical therapy. I felt like I was learning how to walk all over again. I went from wheelchair, crutches, walker to cane in a matter of 8 months. I was the ice queen for almost a year after the injury. The swelling was out of control at times and ice would be the only thing to deflate it. However, I was determined to get moving. Breaking my ankle was an emotional and physically painful process, but it allowed me see how strong I am and how determination & relentless action is the key to success.

There were many times I just wanted to give up on school and physical therapy during this unfortunate time in my life. Sometimes we don't know how strong we are until we are faced with a battle you know most could not survive without maintaining a "somewhat" sound mind and still come out on top.

Time to Slay:

- What's a situation in your life which you displayed tenacity? You were resilient and could have given up, but you kept your eye on the prize

- It's very typical to be strong in one area of your life and have room to improve persistence in other areas. Think about the situation which you feel like you have mastered that area and have stuck to your goals. How can you transfer a few of those traits to the area in which you feel you need the most attention? It could be daunting at first but as you analyze the situation more, you will it doesn't require much more different than the area you are mastering. Typically, it's just a tweak to tailor the goal and craft a plan.

Chapter 25
Find the Champion Within

> "Her bounce back game is strong, just wait on it; she'll grow from it all. Never count this woman out." –Sylvester Mcnutt

One of the most tenacious and self-defining journeys I've been on in my entire life and STILL going through is my 13-year journey towards fertility. One of the ways I have been able to cope with it is by owning, accepting and sharing the journey with the world. Realizing that my story is my fuel which has given me more confidence in finding my own champion within. If it wasn't for this unique path, I don't even think I would be writing this book. The foundation of this book is rooted from the attempts at trying to get pregnant. It takes an enormous amount of tenacity to go from one treatment plan to another, new medication protocols, 4 Fertility specialists, and new diagnosis year after year without the outcome you expect.

I've witnessed women who freak out when they can't lose weight in 30 days. I also witnessed other ladies crumble after trying to conceive for only a few months. It's been a very painful journey each month being rejected and basically feeling like you are being told NO you "can't have" that blessing as you witness others blast right past you effortlessly. Or witnessing people be so horrible to their kids and all you can do is look up to God asking,

"Why can't we have that blessing? We would pour so much love and energy into our kids." I've cried many nights and have had much pain on this route.

My ego and self-worth have been affected in the process and there were many times I thought I was a failure. There were times when I felt like I wasn't contributing appropriately to my marriage and not able to provide the one gift a woman can provide to her man. I have felt cursed and bitter. You may not be able to directly relate to my infertility journey. However, during this chapter I want you to start thinking about something you have been wanting for a long-time and you still do not have it: getting married, having a successful business, getting out of debt, medical problem healed, or a specific number on the scale.

You feel like you have been putting all of the efforts and energy needed to get the results you are looking for, but somehow that dream has yet been fulfilled. You feel like giving up at times and frustrated to keep moving forward. This journey I have been experiencing is not by coincidence. It took me 13 years to realize that my ultimate god-giving purpose is for me to be a vessel to deliver this message to all women across the world: stay tenacious on your journey towards your dreams no matter what! If you can't stop thinking about it, don't stop working for it. So, here's my infertility story. Not even my closest friends know everything. I tend to not talk about the frustrations of the process because I always have the "happy" mask on top of the deep wounds and frustrations. What I learned this year is that my story is my fuel!

I met my husband Josh at church in youth group. It's a funny story how we started dating because I wasn't even attracted to him at first sight. When I first started going to the church my friend Sulai invited me to in 6th grade. Josh was one the first people who helped me navigate through the sections of the church. As I began to get to know everyone and make friends this unfamiliar place which frightened me at first glance became my second home. I started going to church every Wednesday and Sunday plus ALL of the youth group outings. I was going so much that my mom decided to give a visit to the place which I talked about all the time. During her first visit Josh was starring in a play "Arch the Angel" and he was wearing this brown leather "s-medium" (too small) jacket hopping across the stage with so much energy and animation. My mom saw him and said, "I like him, that's going to be my son-in-law one day". Now, at this time I was 14 years old. So, first off, I was NOT even thinking about marriage and my 2nd objection was my friends in youth group thought Josh (at that time) was a nerd. I was still wearing a lot of masks, so I didn't really have my own single identity and would turn into a chameleon when around others. So, when my friends didn't like Josh, I felt pressured to agree and overlook him. Not even the words my mom proclaimed over my life took root into my heart. I was a people-pleaser and just went with the flow. Some weeks later, we had a car wash and somehow Josh and I started playing with the bubbles and tossing them at each other in a flirtatious manner. I wasn't even seeing the "nerd" in him anymore. I remember the sun catching his hazel light eyes and chocolate skin and I began to feel a little giddy.

We immediately started building our relationship, but I don't really remember how we established an *official* relationship. I know it all began as friends first then we gradually started to court each other. He proposed to me right after we graduated High School (July 2002) at the Metro Parks in Ohio. We frequently go to that same spot to re-spark those memories of our special day. I knew he was going to propose because we were talking about our future plans and how I was going to Kent State University and he was going to the Art Institute in PA. On the day, he proposed to me, I provided him a promise ring. It was so cute and so aligned. When we became married, we didn't use any contraceptives since we had full intentions on getting pregnant soon. During our first year of marriage, we did get pregnant. It was a surprise. I went to the doctor not feeling well and the doctor came back into room to announce that we were pregnant. We were overjoyed and shocked how fast this was happening.

We had just moved to Tacoma, WA after Josh joined the United States Air Force in Nov 2002. So we were a poor young couple and were about to announce to our family that we are expecting our first child. Then we get a phone call from the same doctor stating he made a mistake and that I WAS pregnant and my HCG levels were high, but when he compared the date I was on cycle, he realized I miscarried. We were sad, but not majorly depressed or anything. We were shocked that it happened and were eager to try again. Many months went by; I tried using ovulation predictors with no luck, basal thermometers with no luck. Soon it was 2 years that passed by and we were not able to get pregnant again. Sex began to feel rehearsed and passionless.

All we were doing was trying to build a family and completely forgot about connecting with one another. I remember us going to our first married couples retreat around our 2nd year of marriage and really got reconnected and told ourselves that we will no longer make "getting pregnant" our focus. We started building a great foundation with each other and felt very much in love. We were approaching our 5th wedding anniversary and were still not pregnant. In those years, we didn't talk about kids much, but we BOTH knew it was our desire and dream. It was just so painful to discuss and we buried deep within our hearts that even we couldn't see it or touch it.

So, you know others didn't think nothing of it either. Can you relate? This dream you have is on your mind almost every day, you walk around as if nothing is affecting you, but when you get alone and allow your mind to wonder it stings and hurts so bad knowing you have not achieved your desire as of yet.

After our 5th year wedding anniversary we decided to see our first Fertility Specialist. We knew something had to be wrong. We felt so left out as people our age were having kids every day and our family on the Stepteau side was growing by the minute. We both had every hormone and reproductive test conventional medicine would do and they found nothing. The doctors kept saying we were perfectly normal and all we can think about is, "if we are normal, why are we not parents as of yet?" At times, we were hoping to find a diagnosis to just be able to fix it and move on beyond this chapter of our life. We were beginning to feel like it was a broken old record and tired of hearing the same generic answers with NO results.

Now people were starting to ask us the most annoying questions a couple who is dealing with infertility would be asked, "When are you guys going to start having kids?" Little did people know at that time is that we were trying for almost 7 years. Test after test and medication after medication. Nothing worked! We felt trapped and silenced. Every time we would try to speak to family members or friends they would say a very insensitive comment because they honestly didn't know what to say. We kept hearing the same comments, "Breathe and it will happen", "Drink wine before you have sex", "Go adopt and I bet you get pregnant", "Maybe you should slow down and not work out so much", "I bet you took contraceptives and that's why", "Is it you or Josh?", "Put your legs up after sex and let the sperm get to the egg", or the most horrible comment after I just shared to a family member that I had my 3rd miscarriage that morning they pointed at their child and told asked me, "why would you want one of these? They are super hard work?" I mean we seriously heard it ALL in 13 years and not ONE TIME did anyone in our circle just offer an ear to listen or a shoulder to cry on. Everyone always had their 2 cents to give in solving the solution. Please take some time to think right now about someone in your life who you can just be there for. How can you support them? Don't try to fix their problem or play "God", just be.

We were approaching our 10th year renewal of vows ceremony. I was finally going to experience a real wedding! Right before the event we discovered we were approximately 8 weeks pregnant and planned to announce to our family and friends on the event with an ultrasound pic on a projector screen. I didn't even get to celebrate this news for even a week. I miscarried so quickly and we were sad. However, we were in process of planning our renewal of vows ceremony and the show had to keep going.

This is when it became more depressing and frustrating. We all have our limits and this segment of the infertility journey was my breaking point. Remember my rubber band analogy? Well I felt like the rubber band snapped and there was no option to upgrade or to obtain another band. Hubby deployed with military for 9 months which was complicated in itself, but I managed to keep busy with a few goals (Fitness Competitions & Business). When he returned back home we conceived within the first 60days of him being back home and miscarried at 6 weeks.

Between that and other stressors, I went into deep depression. I was tired of not feeling like I wasn't good enough. I began to feel very resentful towards God. I thought several times to just run into a tree with my car to end it all, but I held on. I even asked my hubby for a divorce thinking I wasn't good enough for him. Then something hit me around Sept of last year. I was reminded of how tenacious I've been through other trials in my life (my husband gave me a wakeup call which I will discuss in an upcoming chapter) and I started to read affirmations to myself and pull myself out of the dark hole. Life began to look fresh and exciting! My marriage thriving and so many blessings going on around us. The beginning of 2016, I totally let go of the thought of motherhood. I told myself that I will ENJOY my journey and my empty nest. I will do all of the things people with kids couldn't do.

We moved into an urban apartment close to downtown which I walk to work each day. I had parties on the rooftop on weeknights, and just enjoyed life. March 2016, I knew I was pregnant again and didn't even test or go see a doctor. I just know my body after all of these years and had another miscarriage. It honestly didn't even phase me because I know I have a purpose to help change the mindset of women around the world. I haven't given up on this journey towards motherhood, but I am moving forward with a different mindset.

Time to Slay:

- How can you have a different mindset about the dream you are waiting for?

- How can you enjoy the journey more?

-
- When we get so fixated on the end goal we lose track of the journey.
- How can you display more gratitude on where you are at so far on the journey?
- In some cases, we can't control the outcome, but we always control how we feel and act on the journey.

Chapter 26
Importance of your Environment

> "When your room is clean and uncluttered, you have no choice but to examine your inner state."
> –Marie Kundo

Sometimes the best things to do to move forward is to have a fresh start in the physical and emotional realm. One of the things which helped me declutter my life is by reading the book "The Life-Changing Magic of Tyding Up" by Marie Kundo. The resource is so powerful and insightful on how your environment can affect your level of tenacity and abundance. The main focus on resources encouraged readers to envision their ideal lives and only keep items in your home which spark joy. This practice will help you to find yourself and gain clarity. Marie shares tips on how to let go of guilt so that you don't feel forced to keep stuff, this activity will show you what you really need and what you truly energetically connect with to provide joy. When you perform all her steps, you will be completely surrounded by the things you only love.

Kundo explains to start with your books and materials in the home then your clothing, and to keep going from there. The most important step in the process is to pick the items up one-by-one and ask yourself "Does this spark joy?" If it doesn't, then you immediately discard the item. There are no ifs, ands, or buts; just a simple "yes" or "no" question. I took this concept to another level and started to apply this to my business model, circle of friends, my thoughts, my finances, and heck, even people who follow me on social media. I kept asking myself, "does any of these things spark joy"? I asked myself this question for a series of days and started removing the clutter out of my way to live the life so that I can put energy into the things which DO spark joy in my life.

After reading this book I realized I was holding myself back from my highest potential and bogged down by unnecessary items surrounding with "ok" energy. I started de-cluttering and releasing old items from my life to make room for new things.

> **"I now release all that I no longer need: things, ideas, habits, relationships. I make new for the new to come bursting forth in my life." – Louise Hay**

The environment you allow yourself to be exposed to tends to influence you so subtly that its effects on you may seem as if to arise from some unknown, invisible source. The source is not invisible; on the contrary, it is more noticeable than you think — our environment includes everything that you see, hear, smell, taste and feel around you.

Our environment affects us on a profound level. The negative effects that may seem insignificant may have a major impact on our psyche, our outlook on life and our mood is rather surprisingly manner. For example, your place of residency: is it simply a place where you eat, sleep, and work? Or is it a place you call home?

Subtle factors in our environment have an impact on the way that we feel. The colors of our walls, the colors and patterns of our furniture, the smell in the air, the lack of or the buildup of dust, all affects us; the issue is that this impact usually is not felt for an extended period of time post-exposure. It can also involve the placement of furniture in your home, such as Fung Shui, a Chinese system for arranging your surroundings in harmony and balance with the natural world around you. The wisdom in the practice emphasize direction and placement of furniture actually has an impact on our mood, good health, prosperity, and energy.

Even then, we often will find ourselves unhappy and not understanding why — tending to point our fingers at everything but the surroundings we have placed ourselves in. These effects will most certainly vary from individual to individual.

It is likely that some of us have a higher tolerance to dirt and germs than others. I know people who can't think straight with noise and there are others who desperately need music or background sounds to help concentrate. I have even heard stories of people that function better when their living rooms are in complete disarray. I call that organized chaos. I am not one of those people and there are others who can't stand being in their home until every dish in the sink has been put away in the cupboards and bed made.

Our minds can become naturally very cluttered themselves, having decades of thoughts and memories haunting us on a daily basis. If our environment mirrors this chaos, our senses picking up on the outer chaos will likely only magnify our inner chaos and gremlins. The way I see it is like this: while our minds usually act as escapes from the craziness that is our lives and those things and people that we surround ourselves with, the very same can be said about our environments.

When our minds are overwhelmed by what life throws our way, we can find ourselves in desperate need of calming — our environment can be a safe-haven away from our own inner gremlins. If we cannot find peace from within ourselves, our only option is to look outside of us for answers, for direction and for peace. Imagine yourself coming home from a very bad day.
Things just didn't go right; you were late for work, your boss gave you a very hard time regarding several projects, your spouse is not able to help and console, you call a friend and she is overwhelmed by her own day. You finally arrive home to your safe haven? What will give you more peace? A clean, neat, refreshing-smelling home or a cluttered environment with dishes filling the sink, dog hair all over the couch, and counters are piled with items from weeks ago?

Our homes play a larger role than simply being a place where we go to sleep and watch TV. It should be the place to escape all the negativity from the world which may come your way throughout your days. In fact, it can work in one of two ways: your home can function as a place that allows you to keep you calm and minimize your stress, or it can work as a catalyst for it.

Our environment represents more than just our home — it goes for everything and anything that surround us. The city we live in. The place that we work. Our friends and our family. Everything and everyone that we come into contact with affects us in one way or another — regardless of whether or not we are conscious of the effect.

> **"The space in which we live should be for the person we are becoming now, not for the person we were in the past."-Marie Kundo**

Time to Slay:

- How can you clear out your environment for success?
- What are some relationships, habits, blocks you can let go of that are not serving you well on your journey?
- How will you ensure you proceed with these desires and not shrink or second guess yourself?

Chapter 27

Earth Angel to the Rescue

> "I have a theory that as long as you have one good friend, one real friend, you can get through anything."- Dana Reinhardt

I had my 3rd miscarriage after my husband returned back home from a 9-month deployment and started to mentally shrink. From there, depression started to creep back up. It was like I was completely blocking every blessing I could possibly obtain. I went from an 83% closing rate for discovery calls to 0% during a 3-month period in my online weight management business. I had approximately 20 calls during that time frame and couldn't close one single deal with prospective clients. I started to really freak out then my husband learned that his company was bought by another organization in Renton, WA. Which will result in the lost of his job within 60days.

We were lost and of course beyond frustrated. I felt like we couldn't catch a break. We had literally just bounced back from the period of time we both didn't have any income (only a full year had passed). As the fear began to creep up along with the pressure, my business crumbled. I started getting very depressed and so beyond disappointed in myself. I felt like a failure. I had relocated us to GA, hated the job opportunity then resigned without any income in home to start my own online business and now was ready to quit that as well. I cried almost every day and started drinking rum multiple times a day to soothe the pain. I would be drunk when my husband returned home and very sad.

There were a few peaks of happiness when I would dig super deep but a lot of gray days. I took a five-month sabbatical from social media. Those 5 months were me throwing fits in the house, being drunk, and crying. My very supportive husband didn't know what to do. I started talking crazy and saying, "I'm not good enough for him." I asked him for a divorce several times. He was such a good man to me, patient and comforting.

And I couldn't figure out how to get my 'ish together and stick to something for at least 1 year. I felt lame and he didn't deserve this type of woman. I stopped cooking and cleaning, I just laid around feeling very sorry for myself. I also felt like *well I can't give him a child so why even be together*. Isn't a marriage based on a foundation of building your legacy and your own family together? After 3 natural miscarriages, uncounted medicated cycles with Letrozole and Clomid, failed IVF, and IUI, I couldn't even find faith or hope in this situation anymore. I wanted a divorce and I wanted to die. I really didn't see the purpose of living anymore at this time.

One day my husband grabbed me and said, "We are going to the park right now" with a stern voice. Naturally my husband is a comforting and silly guy so I knew he was serious. He firmly grabbed my hand and basically pulled me into the car. I didn't even have time to resist or even question what he was doing. When I got in the car, it was awkward silence and tension in the air. I asked, "What is going on?" He said "I just want to go to the park." The park was about 15 mins away. As we drove, all I could think about is how upset he was with me.

I knew deep down inside, he had enough and was tired of seeing me drag around with no life. This was almost a period of 5 months and he kept loving on me every day, would ask me if I wanted a smoothie for dinner from Smoothie king or pick up salads for me from Chick-fila. And I felt like his love and patience had reached their own breaking point.

But this day at the pond, I will never forget the passion in his eyes and the assertiveness in his voice. He even had beads of sweat on his forehead from the Georgia heat. He jumped right into conversation and told me, "it doesn't matter that you can't bare me a child, I don't care about you having cooked meals ready when I come home or a clean house, what I do care about is having you in my life." I could see the tears in his eyes and I couldn't help but to start crying myself. He further explained that I am his world and he couldn't see life without me. If I left him, he would want to leave this world as well. He reminded me of the fighter I am. He reflected on other stories that showed how strong I am and the tenacity I have deep down inside of me that pushes through NO MATTER WHAT.

In addition, he reminded me that this is all a test for me during this period of my life. That speech moved me so much. I started to truly feel a bit stronger. As I was crying, I saw a beautiful and vibrant yellow and black butterfly just swarming around me as if it was telling me something. It laid on my knee for a second and I felt this overwhelming surge of love as if someone was hugging me. I cried so hard and my husband wrapped me in his arms. I told him I am so sorry for making his life a little gray and thanked him for holding on to me when I didn't really want to hold on to myself. I told him our life will never be the same.

> "The best place in the world is in the arms of someone who will not only hold you at you best, but will pick you up and hug you tight at your weakest moment." – Unknown

There is power in support. We need people in our circle who will tell us straight up how they feel and tell us straight up if we need an assertive reminder to get your 'ish in order. I am forever thankful for that conversation because it really did remind me of my tenacity and also helped me to truly relate to others who go into deep depression and feel hopeless. This is part of my story and it is a gift to lean on someone when that story becomes difficult.

Time to Slay:

- Who is your life has been your earth angel? How have they impacted your life?
- How can you be someone's earth angel?

Chapter 28
Who's your Tribe?

> "Surround yourself with the doers the believers and thinkers but most of all surround yourself with those who see greatness within you."- Edmund Lee

I never valued the importance of support due to how I was raised and all the emotional trauma I experienced. I was taught to rely on just myself and that God blesses the child who can do for their own. Independency was a huge thing in my home. I do understand, in my mom's defense, she was kicked out of her home at the age of 16. She had to survive the streets of Cleveland as a very young lady. In her world, she was protecting us from the sad disappointments of depending and relying on others for assistance. From my mom's perspective, she had no support from family and taught my sister and I to basically never trust anyone or rely on anyone for help.

This mindset made me feel like a failure when I needed help. I have bust my butt, lost a lot of money, and been in many circles because I have had refused to ask for support. I remember times at church when people offer to pray for me or ask if I needed anything and I would say, "I'm good". Knowing deep down I would love for them to pray for me. I would cry on my own regretting that I denied comfort from another person. However, on the outside you would have never known it was affecting me.

Breaking that cycle took decades to remove. It wasn't until recently that it dawned on me that support is everything.

You are who you surround yourself with. Don't think you can do this alone. You need a tribe of people rallying around you. You need a mentor and someone to challenge you to think outside the box. I didn't get where I am today without support. I've hired coaches, signed up for courses, and reached out to close family/friends when needed. However, always be mindful of who is in your circle.

Be selective with your choice of support, it's a privilege for people to share in your journey and vice versa. We are the people who we are around. It's easy to start exchanging habits with little things like a phrase we tend not to really pay attention to. Next thing you know, you are finding yourself doing something they would do, picking up on the same attitude, and taking interest in the same things.

None of those have to have a negative connotation to it, if you are selective with your tribe. We should have people in our lives we invest in, who pour into our life, and who are on the same level that you can walk through the journey of life with. There is nothing wrong with having lots of acquaintances, as long as you are spending the most time with your inner circle who points you in the right direction.

The other important aspect to keep the momentum in your unstoppable journey is to connect with a tribe of people who will support you. Here are the type of people you need in your circle:

Who Do You Talk to? We all need a support system, an inner circle of people who will give us honest advice and feedback both positive and negative. We all need to have a few people who genuinely want us to do well and who we can rely on. People we can turn to when we face seemingly overwhelming challenges.

Who Do You Go to when Times are Tough? Sharing the load on a bad day or the joy of a good day is a vital ingredient to our wellbeing.

Who is Holding You Accountable?
Having an inner circle has so many benefits: someone you can go to for wise, objective counsel to help you with the many challenges you will face in life. In addition, this person helps you be accountable to your goals

Do you Have an Inner Circle? If not, I highly recommend that you start building one today!

Time to Slay:

Here are a few questions to use to analyze your current tribe or inner circle: Are they encouraging you to chase after your dreams, or are they holding you back from your potential? Are they there to hold your hand through the rough times and point you to God or help you find other ways to suppress the pain? Are they the ones you can trust, or are they the ones hiding something from you?

- Find people who know you well and understand your purpose.
- Choose people who genuinely care enough about you to hold you accountable.
- Speak to people who are successful and motivated in their own right and choose positive people who won't erode your confidence. Leave the naysayers behind.

Chapter 29
Fail Forward

> "Twenty years from now, you will be more disappointed by the things that you didn't do than by the ones you did do, so throw off the bowlines, sail away from safe harbor, and catch the trade winds in your sails. Explore, Dream, Discover."
>
> – Mark Twain

Have you ever done something so crazy or stupid on the spur of moment based on emotions then regret doing it very soon after making the final decision? I have a great story to share which had my home with 0 income for almost 6months. Yes, you read it right NO INCOME from my husband nor I. It was a period of our life which was full of uncertainty. I accepted a role in Georgia including a full relocation package making $70,000/yr. salary as a Sr. Buyer. You couldn't tell me nothing, I knew I arrived to success. We rented a 3000 sq.ft. home. I thought I was this big shot supply chain professional who was unstoppable.

Within 30 days, I started seeing this was all a mistake. I couldn't believe I relocated my husband and I from Ohio to Georgia to a role which sparked NO joy whatsoever for me. On my first day, I arrived to meet my direct supervisor who was dressed in nurse scrubs. I was appalled and very confused. I was told I would have my own office and they gave me this impression that my role was working closely with the Director of Innovation Material, not a manufacturing worker. So, when I saw this lady in nurse scrubs sitting right at materials/manufacturing section of the plant, I became overwhelmed with frustration.

On my first day, my supervisor texted me while on lunch stating she was going to fire my subordinate (a material coordinator) because she smells like cigarette smoke. I knew right then and there that this lady was going to be trouble and knew this was going to be an interesting roller coaster ride.

I tried to stay as positive as I could since I just signed a lease paying $1400 a month for a large home and just relocated over 700 miles away from Ohio. My husband was even finished with his role back in Ohio during this time. He had put in his 2 weeks' notice to join me in Georgia. As each month went by, the relationship between my supervisor and I became even more intense. She would constantly talk about people behind their backs and play very petty games with manufacturing staff. Her nonsense was beyond my morals and value (in a negative way).

I decided to speak to her since communication is everything to me and I didn't want to speak about her behind her back. Our first conversation went HORRIBLE. She was so defensive and said I was trying to be the boss. All I did was suggest we read a book together -- Type Talk at Work-How the 16 Personality Types Determine Your Success on the Job – a book which we can get to know each other's strengths and weaknesses. I wanted harmony I knew that I saw her more than my own husband and peace in this environment would help us both out in an enormous way. I continually strived to work super hard to get her approval

or try to excel at the work, but I was struggling to keep up with the fast-paced environment.
I was working 60 plus hours a week trying to stay ahead of the game. I was making mistake after mistake with purchasing orders and shipments. As my employee moral decreased so did my performance. I found myself crying in the car in the parking lot before work and during lunch trembling with nervousness and fear. I felt so guilty and stupid for accepting this role. My husband didn't obtain work as of yet in GA because we had intentions of him going to school full-time to become a graphic designer. 8 months had passed by and I was beyond miserable.

I made the tough decision to speak to HR regarding the tensions and a possible transfer into another department since I felt like my performance was immensely declining. HR manager explained to me that in my contract it states that I need to stay in the role for 24 months before any transfers. I thought to myself, how the hell will I be able to put up with this crazy boss and this role for another 16 months? Somehow my boss got notice that I went to HR and she blew up on me. I knew I couldn't take this abuse any longer so I called my husband and asked him if I could put in my two weeks' notice. My husband knew how miserable I was and as usual, my husband supported me in the decision and I quit the job. I was scared and happy all at the same time.

This was the biggest faith move I have EVER made in my entire adult life. I quit a job knowing there was NO income in the house at all with a $1400 rent payment due each month. Whew! It took almost 6 months for us to get some stable income in the home. Those were the most nerve-wracking and stressful 6 months of my life! So much uncertainty. I had NO peace always on the edge, always stressed, but had to put a smile on my face and try to make ends meet with my business "Fit4Life". I remember I was so desperate my first offer was $100 for ONE MONTH of virtual coaching (1hr weekly calls/weekly customized meal plans/fitness plans). Talk about devaluing yourself, but I did get 11 new clients and paid rent that month.

> **"There will be a time, not so far from now, that you will look back on this phase of your life and instead of condemning it or beating up on it...Instead of blaming or guilting, you will feel appreciation for it, because you will understand that the renewed desire for life was born out of this time period that will bring you to physical heights that you could not achieved without the contrast that gave birth to this desire." -Abraham Hicks**

We reached out to several people to borrow money. We even lost a few friends in this process because we asked them for money. We were DESPERATE. We pawned my 2-carat diamond wedding ring and other items in the house to make ends meet. I felt too guilty to pray because I knew I did this to our family. I kept thinking, "Why would I do this? If I could have stuck it out a little longer to find another job, we wouldn't be struggling so much right now." I couldn't even talk to anyone because I felt as though no one would feel sorry for me since I made this dumb decision. Can you relate?

It took me some years to fully forgive myself for getting us trapped in a situation like this. It pops up very often and I must constantly silence the gremlins. The way I constantly reframe my thinking to forgive myself is to give myself permission to fail forward. As I reflect, my "desperation" pushed me to start my own business. I started sharing my story and setting myself on social media as the expert in Health & Wellness. After consistent & tenacious efforts, I started bringing in consistent income equivalent to my salary as a Sr. Buyer in that Supply Chain. Plus, hubby was offered a very nice role during that time.

John Maxwell has an amazing book if you are struggling with moving forward after you fail. It's called *Fail Forward*. So much application and revelation in this book which I reference back to often as I continue to make mistakes and learn on this journey. The biggest call-to action from the book is to figure out how to turn your mistakes into stepping stones for success.

Time to Slay:

- What can you forgive yourself for? How will you go about this process?

- Do you need to forgive someone in your life? How will you communicate with them your emotions?

- How can forgiveness propel you forward in your journey?

Chapter 30

Purify your Heart: Let Go of Bitterness

> "Whatever purifies you, is the correct road."- Rumi

For years, I never understood why my father couldn't be a part of my life. He tried several times. His first attempt that I could remember is when I was about to become a teenager. He came into my life and said he wanted a relationship. He invited me to his church with his newborn daughter (my sister) and her mom. They looked like a happy family. It was hard to not become jealous. The baby burped and he quickly grabbed a wipe and whipped to clean her up and he held her during the service with so much love and joy. I became sad thinking, "why does he take care of his new born baby and not me?"

All the years we lost that chance to be connected in the same way. I always thought about how it would feel to have a man embrace you without abusing you. I wanted that innocent unconditional love from a man. I wanted to be daddy's little girl. So many layers of anger and bitterness overwhelmed me. I tried to be optimistic by telling myself that at least he wants a relationship now. After visiting his church and meeting my new sister he called me a few times and then he disappeared. I thought he died or something. I became angry with him. I began to ask myself, "what is wrong with me?" Remnants of that hurt showed in my life as I grew up.

Fast forward a bit, my first year of college I ran into my father's other child who is about 1 year younger than me. At this point in time I haven't heard or spoken to my father for 6 years. She shared with me how he is in her life and helping her with college expenses and such. Of course, this added to my anger. I couldn't believe he had ANOTHER child that he took care of. He had 3 daughters. I am the oldest and he basically forgot about me. How could I not feel angry? I was so confused and called my mom. She tried to be nice about it. I have to say; my mom has never discouraged me to have a relationship with my father. She never really spoke down about him. It was always me upset at him. My parents go way back, they were high-school sweethearts and were dating off and on from the time she was a young teenager until she had me at the age of 21. I always thought it would have been a perfect scenario if they would get back together and we could be a happy family.

Since then he has tried to come back into my life 2 times. These two times I was a married woman with a loving and VERY supportive husband. At the surface, I thought who cares I don't need him and he doesn't get to me anymore but every time I think of the possibilities of having a father daughter relationship I get flooded with emotions. One year while I was married I just let him have it. I told him, he will either be in my life or OUT. I angrily shared with him that I don't have time for the games nor the emotional roller coaster rides anymore. This stuff hurts. I want to move forward with consistency.

He instantly called my mother and said, "Erica wasn't playing and she means business. Where does she get that spark from?" He arranged a time for us to go get ice cream. I thought it would be just us two, but he invited my mom, sister and baby brother. I was turned off and aggravated. He sensed the emotions and didn't connect with me again until a few years later. On my 29th Birthday, he offered to take me to a nice upscale restaurant located in Lakewood, Ohio and I accepted because regardless of all the irritations and pain he has added to my life, I whole-heartedly desired a relationship with him. We actually had a good time and I believe it sparked something different. I began to let down my guards and I bought him a ticket to attend with me alone on a train ride Father's Day 2013; to me this was a perfect time to rekindle some things and to continue to grow our connection and have that father-daughter relationship I always dreamed of. I even took our picture we took together at my 29th Birthday celebration dinner and put it in a frame to give to him as a gift. I was so beyond excited about this anticipated time together.

I talked about it all week and my husband was excited for me as well. My father called me and cancelled the same day saying he got into a fender bender and was a bit stressed about it. I get an accident can be frustrating, but in my head, I was like *"you still breathing, right?"* I didn't sense any urgency from him to make our outing happen. If he wanted to do this, he would have figured out the details. Then to add to the anger I logged into Facebook some hours later seeing he was tagged at his Dad's house by other family members with the crispest outfit on: brand new bright white sneakers, white shorts and the sharpest plaid button up shirt. To me, he didn't look stressed from his "fender bender" nor concerned that he put me on the back-burner once again. I cried so hard, and guess who had to console me: my loving and supportive husband. I really believed this was the last straw with me and I can tell my husband wasn't too happy with him either at this point. This time he hurt two people.

I started having a relationship with my Aunt (my father's sister) and I think he became a bit jealous. He came to my 30th birthday celebration and gave me $100 in cash. I thanked him for it, but never desired money from him. All I wanted for 3 decades of my life was his heart and his time. I felt like he gave me the money out of pity. Money does NOT buy my happiness. Some months later he sent me $300 and I thanked him. I know deep down in my heart he is confused on how to be a dad in my life. I appreciate his attempts. His father (my grandfather) wasn't 100% present in his life as a child; unfortunately, because of lack of the knowledge, the cycle continued.

I eventually moved on, but didn't truly heal the deeper wounds. I let go of the dream of having a relationship with my father. I do not hate him; I just don't get caught up on the childhood dream of having a family. We haven't spoken since that time and not until recently I totally released the broken wounds and hurt from this situation. I really do think that is why I've been blessed with my husband; I needed a man who could show me that I was worthy of unconditional love to combat the belief that I was just for men to ignore or take advantage of. I started expressing gratitude to God that I was blessed with an awesome husband. I know many ladies who don't have as supportive and loving husband as mine. I stepped in a new realm in my heart; accepting my path as I continually move forward towards my destiny.

Remember, sometimes things won't be completely resolved or fixed. However, this doesn't mean you can't free yourself from bitterness.

These has been some very dark wounds I had to remove layer by layer. I am always a continuous work in progress. I call myself a "life-long learner". Here are the ways I continue to tear down the walls of bitterness/anger:

Time to Slay:

- Identify if you suppress your anger/bitterness or do you vent/release at the onset of emotion. Realize that both methods have its cons. Analyze how you react to your situation. Suppressing anger/bitterness will begin to leak into other areas in your life. Venting and releasing anger/bitterness is typically considered "gossip". Are you telling a trusted friend or loved one to help you be rational or are you just venting to have someone agree with you?

- Write down your angry and emotion (Deeply ingrained hurts and pain) Writing this story has made we understand my emotions attached to this pain. Explaining how my father picked me up and dropped me more than one time reveals the tenacity in me.

You can also do an emotional income expense sheet:

- **Emotional Income Expense sheet**
  Asset/Deficiencies
  A) Write them down from the last few days to get a better understanding of how you spend your "emotions".
  B) At the onset of a trigger to your unpleasant emotion take a moment to take in a deep breath. Take a step back for five minutes to gather your thoughts and analyze your emotions. Become more mindful on how to react and respond to stressful moments throughout your day.

- **Neutralize Emotional Projections/Reframe:**
  Try deep breathing a few times a day to gain more and flow in your thinking. Focus on your heart as you breathe in. Concentrate on a positive feeling or attitude as you breathe out. Lock in this new feeling as you continue to breathe it in and out through your heart.

This routine is guaranteed to shift you out of a negative emotional state into a positive one. The situation with my father took some soul searching and self-love to move forward. I am at peace to view this situation in a different light now. My father's father wasn't the most active in his life. He didn't have a template or foundation to understand or value the role of a father. He didn't receive the blueprint on how to be in my life without feeling like giving me money. He didn't know how to love me beyond gifts. I no longer point my fingers at him blaming him. I thank him for the opportunity to endure such a thing to make me the person I am today. I no longer trash talk him. He is my father and he will always have some level of love from me. He doesn't know any better so how can I hold him accountable to those unachievable expectations. How can you neutralize your emotions with a hurtful situation? What thoughts can you replace in your heart to come to peace? How can you move forward and let go of the anger?

Chapter 31

What's your Money Story?

> "Owning your story is the bravest thing you will ever do." – Brene Brown

During my childhood, my family would gather at my grandparents' home to bring in the New Year. This particular year was no different than other years, there was a ton of food in the kitchen including my grandfather's delicious ribs with his amazing homemade barbeque sauce. My uncles were in the backyard firing their guns, and a group of other family members were gambling on my grandparents' slot machine in their living room and playing Pokeno at the dining room table.

Our family favorite method to gamble with one another was playing Pokeno. It's a hybrid of poker and bingo played with a 52-card deck. Each player is given a Pokeno board, similar to a bingo card consisting of 25 squares (Five rows each with five squares). A dealer gradually uncovers and announces each card of the deck, with players attempting to complete a row of five cards using counters to cover each card on the board as it is announced. My family would take it to the next level and have money pots for following additional accomplishments: 4 corners, Center, 4 of a kind, and of course Pokeno (5 across, down, or diagonally). Typically, they would use coins to put in the "pot"; each game could cost a quarter, dime, or even a penny for each Pokeno board you have with each game. Everything depending on what the dealer declares before the round starts. Some family members would have as many as 5 boards at a time.

This was a symbolic year for me; I was finally old enough to gamble with the family (approximately 14 years old). The feeling was surreal; I had watched from the sidelines for years as everyone played and left the table with buckets of money. I would dream about what I would buy with the money. One of my dreams was to buy a pair of Michael Jordan tennis shoes since I was playing basketball at the time. I would imagine getting a red, black, and white pair and how those shoes would give me the speed and hops I needed to effectively play on my team. I felt giddy and super excited to await my turn for a chance to make my dream come true. After a few people dropped out of the game, I was asked if I wanted to join. I anxiously said, "Yes!" Then I straightened up my voice to act cool and calm because in my head I was thinking, adults don't get this excited to play Pokeno. I had to make sure I was blending in and not being too anxious.

When I sat in the hot seat instantly an overwhelming feeling hit me. I was thinking to myself *wow, this time I am hanging out with the 'big dawgs'*. I felt powerful and over the moon. My heart was racing and my knees were shaking. I was emulating everything I had witnessed through the years. If you were a fly on the wall you would see me grinning ear to ear with beads of sweat on my top lip and forehead as I began to get into the game. We were playing for a while (approximately 30mins or so) and actually having fun. Everyone was laughing and making fun of each other on their losses and celebrating their wins. You could probably hear all the laughter and chatter several houses away. My younger cousins and sister were running around playing with one another on the first floor of the home and in the basement. The aroma of grandpa's sauce filled the home along with the other typical foods of greens, mac & cheese, yams, and dessert.

We continued to play Pokeno as the money pots for 4 corners and 4 of a kind built up. The game ends when someone gets Pokeno (5 across, down, or diagonally). If no one win the other pots, then it just rolls over to the next game. We were playing for quarters and it had to be a few hours at this point because the 4-corner pot was overflowing; it had to be at least $50-60 worth of quarters in the pot. I just knew that amount could cover my Jordan's. As we continued to play, the concentration increased among the group. The room began to silence more as we intensely awaited the cards to be called out by the dealer, as we all sat back withheld breaths and sweaty foreheads.

I was one card away and just waited silently for my King of hearts to be called. About 3 seconds later, my card was called and I hesitated because I wanted to make sure I was calling out the right win before shouting "4 corners!" out loud. I spoke up the next card was being called at the same time, and I said, "Wait…hey, I got 4 corners"! A family member said to me with no thought or remorse, "well you missed your chance, you shouldn't be so slow. The next card is already called and I have 4 corners, so the money is mine." I was crushed, I even pleaded with the family member and explained that we called out at the same exact time. My mom even tried to defend me and an argument started over the money. I couldn't believe that a family member twice my age would even be so aggressive with me over that pot of money. My Jordan dream was crushed right at that moment. From this moment on, this story shaped how I ran my personal finances and how I felt about money.

After the incident with my family, I vowed to never gamble again. Isn't it funny when we declare such a bold statement and find ourselves still falling in the trap? My whole life I have gambled with money, but in a very different way than expected. This revelation came to me through a coaching session with a fellow life coach. Prior to our call, I had already done some inner work on identifying that this story from my childhood had indeed created my money story. I just didn't connect the dots to how I had taken on the gambling mindset for over 15 years in my own personal finances. As my coach asked the right questions, she helped me intuitively define that I was acting out my worst fear.

Gambling. Merriam-Webster defines to gamble as a risky action in the hope of a desired result; a game of chance for money; to bet on an uncertain outcome; to stake something on a contingency: take a chance.

When I approached the table to join my family for my first round of gambling, I felt empowered, on cloud 9, and excited about what money could provide me: my Jordan's. When the dream was taken from me I began to feel powerless, devalued, and very frustrated about money. These same traits have carried on in my adult life. I basically "gambled" my finances from one check to another because it gave me a rush and a huge thrill and helped me escape my frustrations with money. I wasn't in a casino gambling my money, but I had a "gambler's mindset". Most of my adult life I frowned upon budgets, or any organization with money.

Each year I would say, "I need to take control over my finances." I would invest in every financial guru's program I could find such as Dave Ramsey, Suze Orman, or Robert Kiyosaki. My husband and I would create budgets and not even one month later, we would be derailed with an unexpected purchase or bill. Then the vicious cycle began, the emotions from the Pokeno table with my family arises and I would begin to self-sabotage to cope with the mistakes or lack of funds. Typically overspending would be the way I would cope with financial woes. It took me a longtime to realize this, but every time I would have a financial setback it would feel just like that moment at the table: the feelings of lack of power, overwhelm, and frustration.

We tend to give money a lot of power and even give our personal power away to money. I have been through many financial circles because I've allowed the scenario which happened at the age of 14 years old dictate the level of power I felt I had with money. You may not believe this, but for the majority of my adult life, I did not have a concrete budget because I was feeling incapable; I would spend money and it would appear when I needed it. I would put my time in at work or business when needed and then uncontrollably spend almost everything earned in a matter of days (Feast and Famine syndrome).

This is how my money habits correlated with gambling: my choices sometimes all worked out (an unexpected check comes into the mail or a new 90day client books with me) and then sometimes we were left not knowing how to pay rent or other critical living expenses. My husband and I have earned a significant amount of income over the 14 years together and unfortunately we did not have a dime saved for emergencies for a very long time. We took a risk every day with our budget. When emergencies raised, we were completely overwhelmed and frustrated that we were not able to cover the expenses. We ended up borrowing from payday loan companies or family members. We are still a work in progress when it comes to finances, however we are diligently working on removing each layer of our money blocks together so that we live the abundant life we were destined to live.

To attract a steady money-flow in your life, you must learn how to view money not as a thing merely, but as an expression of energy- ultimately, as an expression of your own energy. As I invested the time and energy to explore my feelings and disbeliefs, I realized this story connected heavily to my underlying root issue blocking abundance in my life. I began to do inner work and created reframes for the disbeliefs to clear those blocks.

When my family member called me out at the table that day during the Pokeno game, I felt like I wasn't good enough. So now I constantly remind myself I am indeed enough in every aspect of my life. The healing helped me to trust myself in the process so that I end this feast and famine mindset for good! I now have a much better relationship with money. During a 90-day period I took extra time to uncover my own money story, clear out energy blocks, and started the process of healing the 14year-old girl at the Pokeno table.

Now money is just an exchange of energy and it is very easy to obtain. And in that 90-day period, I obtained $26,939.64 in cash or gifted services. In the "Time to Slay" section of the chapter I have provided the actual tools I used to attract more abundance in my life. Give it a try and use #unstoppabletenacity #timetoslay on social when you start seeing the floodgates open up. Remember, sharing is caring.

Your story may not be the same as mine, but take some time right now and think about your money story. Do you live paycheck to paycheck or client by client and wonder how bills will get paid at times? Do you dread looking at your budget or planning finances? Have you found yourself sabotaging yourself through thoughtless spending habits? Are you tired of hustling for money? If you have been struggling with consistent overflow of abundance in your life and suffering from feast and famine syndrome, it's an underlying root reason why you do what you do. There is a reason for everything. It's your job to undercover the possible culprit which keeps you in this cycle. I will show you how.

> **"Wealth isn't produced out of the ground, or out of the factory. It is produced out of the cosmic 'ground' of being out the infinite 'factory' of ideas". J. Donald Walters –Money Magnetism**

Money Cycle
Core beliefs > Thoughts > Feelings > Actions

Time to Slay:

- What was your earliest memory about money?
- Did your family experience a defining moment around money? A defining moment shapes our beliefs – we take away from that experience a meaning.
- Now write one paragraph…" My current relationship with money is…."
- How is that story still affecting your current money mindset?
- Start a **'Money Journal'** to explore your relationship with money, added value, and outgoing expenses. (download Unstoppable Tenacity money journal here: www.unstoppabletenacity.com
- Download Royalty Clutch Tool Kit www.unstoppabletenacity.com

- Write about what's working, what feels good, and when and where do you feel frustrated and powerless or just not right.
- Track incremental weekly goals to regain power (see money journal above)

Chapter 32

Mastering your Feminine Energy

> "Being strong can also be feminine. I don't think feminine equals being weak. Embracing your fierce tigress energy is very sexy."
> – Erica Stepteau

As a child, I was pretty much a tomboy. I remember climbing fences and hanging out with the boys during my pre-teen years and also during middle school I was on the basketball team. I was super-fast on the court, but couldn't get the ball in the basket for the life of me. Ironically, I had the same basketball coach as my mom when she was in middle school. My mom has several trophies for her basketball accomplishments as a child. She was the starting Guard and I heard the way she handled the ball was unbelievable. Plus, she had quick feet and a great jump shot. So of course, my coach was expecting me to play like mom. Well, at least one of her traits passed down to me. I could definitely handle the ball very well and played great defense.

However, my jump shots were terrible. It's like every time I would throw the ball up it either was way off or bounced right off the rim. My skills didn't discourage me; I was so in love with playing ball, but I found myself not wanting to tap into my feminine energy. I really didn't know then how to "act" like a girl. I felt like I couldn't relate with most of them and felt too strong and powerful to be in their midst. I had in my mind that girls who wore heels and wanted to have pretty nails were "weak".

Due to all the traumatic experiences, I had up until this point, being "strong" was all had in me to do. I was the person who would speak up first, volunteer first, and start a fight first. I wore very baggy jeans and loose tops and my hair cut super short. I don't ever recall wearing a dress nor heals between the ages of 10-13 years old.

There was a shift in me when I entered high school. I began to see the power of femininity and started to wear wedges and even makeup. Even though I was still wearing a few masks during this time still, I began to shed the mask of thinking being feminine was weak.

Femininity is a special gift which should be tapped into more often by women. It makes us softer, gentler, kinder, nurturing, more compassionate, and naturally loving. As women, we are naturally more vulnerable and open. We are created to bond and connect with others in a special way. Many women are wearing many hats throughout the day: Mom, wife, employee, entrepreneur, and all the "inbetween" roles which are needed to execute daily tasks. Most women feel there is no room in their day to be feminine. I would like to help you see you can still be

"wonder woman" and still include femininity.

Foster feminine energy through planned activities such as getting your nails, hair or even having a girls' night out. Foster activities which brings out cool, creative, passive, and compassionate side of you. When you get the chance to participate in these activities, find a way to dress in a way which makes you feel sexy, and fierce. Even if it requires that you get up 15 minutes earlier so you can take care of yourself and look your best so you feel your best.

> **"The recipe for what makes a woman sexy at any age or size is simple: beauty, brains, and class, all served with a healthy dose of confidence and purpose." –Erica Stepteau**

Time to slay:

Tenacious Queen, it's important to walk around with your head held high beaming with confidence. Feeling sexy is a state of mind. With the right mindset, you will definitely be able to get your sexy back! Follow the tips below to master your feminine energy:

Dress in Ways that Make you Feel Good. Be comfortable while showing off your best features. For example, if you have great legs, don't be afraid to dress so people will see them. Don't Hide Behind Loose Clothing - You want to wear clothes that complement you, but you don't want to be so obscure no one will notice.

Find a New Hair Style. There's nothing more satisfying than making one simple change that makes all the difference in the world. Go with something that fits your mood. Add extensions, change the color or do a bold cut.

Buy New Make-up and Create a Whole New Look. It's amazing what a little blush or lipstick can do for the psyche. Concentrate on the eye make-up. The eyes say a lot and it's up to you to determine how you want them to speak to the world. Visit the counter of your favorite makeup brand at a department store and ask the professional there to show you what looks will flatter you and how to achieve them. The professional who works for these brands are often trained make-up artists who have a lot of great advice to give.

Pamper Yourself-Nothing says "Sexy" like a little time set aside for YOU! You'll feel and look better. Get a massage and/or facial every month. This will provide the right environment for the much-needed YOU time. The relaxation will help bring your mind and body to a whole new level. You'll feel great!

Accept Compliments. When someone compliments you, don't come back with a negative response or a half-way acceptance of new feminine energy. Warmly smile and say, "Thank you." Feel proud to be beautiful. Enjoy the compliments. They are simply a recognition that your feminine energy is flowing more freely than before. It means you're bringing your energies back into balance. When you start to allow feminine energy to flow back into your life, people will notice. Remember the client results I shared in a previous chapter? Her husband sensed this new feminine energy and it prompted him to buy flowers for her for the first-time in years.

Chapter 33
Manage Your Sexual Energy

> "Sexual energy and creative energy is the same energy. There are the components of desire and allowing. Those are the two components that must be present in the successful creation of anything."
> – Abraham Hicks

Due to my past sexual abuse, I struggled a lot with sexuality. I have been married basically my whole adult life and have had a hard time tapping into my own unique sexual identity. The first few years of my marriage, I had a very hard time opening up to my husband in this department. Those same emotions I had as a 6-year-old child haunted me when I felt "forced" or "pressured" to have sex. This created a huge wedge into our marriage, but what helped us was our authentic connection and friendship with one another. My glorious husband has had to co-create the process of removing one layer of emotional trauma at a time which I experienced as a child (the molestation and self-worth issues associated with the emotional roller coaster ride with my father). One year it hit me that I could no longer live in the past, I had a wonderful man who had been extremely patient with me and it was time to step into a new level of sexuality. I declared to give my husband my all without resistance. This took a few years and lots of prayer, but soon I started to really trust myself to let go and fully trust my husband.

I started to realize how sexual energy dictates your level of blessings and opportunities. Your sexual energy expands and your ability to give and receive pleasure are multiplied. You become more able to experience higher levels of pleasure, energetic ecstasy, and multiple whole body orgasms. Your experience of sublime union with the Divine also expands.

The connection you have with your spouse or significant other affects your desires and your level of tenacity. Sexual energy is one of the strongest energies known to man. Have you seen a horny cat? I mean she makes it known to the whole neighborhood and some that she is ready and don't you dare stand in her way! A sexually frustrated woman can't attract all the goodness into her life and have unstoppable tenacity. Most people have a hard time connecting the dots. I get asked all the time: how can you connect tenacity with sexual energy?

First of all, sexuality is a huge part of our spiritual being. Sexual energy is POWERFUL. When a woman has an orgasm all of her divine energy flows through every cell of her body. In addition, based on Caroline Robertson, author of *The Sexual Energy Elixir,* she shares how sexual energy has healing powers and the capacity to revitalize specific organs within the body. The therapeutic powers of sexual energy are well documented in many spiritual literatures. When you contain this powerful energy within your body, it automatically moves into healing diseases present in the body.

The force of this sexual energy has the power to burn through resistances within you (that arise from emotional wounds or fears) – "it's like being under the influence of a powerful drug while also being conscious in its wake". Based on research Sen has taken as he shared his points in his blog post titled: *Calm Down Mind*.

Unfortunately, our nation has distorted beliefs when it comes to sex and think our sexual parts are bad or not an important part of well-being. Maybe you detest your sexual organs and have completely shut off this compartment within yourself and realize this is affecting your quality of life and vitality. Maybe you have been emotional disturb by heartaches and pain now you are resistant to fully open this area of your life. You feel trapped and constantly frustrated about how your sex life is going or the lack of activity in your life. Maybe you have become so distorted with the application of your sexual energy that you are using it to control and manipulate others.

If you have been sexually abused then your beliefs and thought patterns are even more altered. I cannot stress how important it is to effectively manage your sexual energy whether you are single or married. "Sexual energy creates a very powerful positive aura in your physical being, which can be sensed by people around you as a "magnetic" quality in your personality. Napoleon Hill, in his book, *Think and Grow Rich* had mentioned that all the influential people that he'd interviewed were ones who had strong sexual natures in them but were also conscious enough to channel this energy into their being", Sen: *Calm Down Mind*. One might think physical release is the only way to manage your sexual desires. However, there are ways to shift these intense feelings into a spiritual awakening and

transformational journey. Instead of focusing on repressing and stuffing your emotions/feelings, try exploring and learning about yourself. Mateo Sol says, "I've learnt that it is never good to repress anything in life.
Repression is another form of postponing, in other words, whatever you repress will eventually catch up to you. **Sexual energy cannot be created or destroyed, it can only be transformed"** from his article: *Transforming Sexual Energy into Spiritual Energy.*

During my coaching encounters with women we get into conversations every single day about how they desire to have a better sex life with their significant others but can't find the time nor are they motivated enough to make it a priority. It's important to learn how to use your sexual energy appropriately in a balanced and loving way to keep your hearts and mind open and cleared to tenaciously move forward towards the life you have always dreamed of.

Time to Slay:

You should understand the importance of managing your sexual energy and the impact it has on your tenacious journey. **This week evaluate your sex life. Don't overlook this subject.**

Journal how you are sexually frustrated whether you are single or married.

- How is it affecting your life as a whole?
- How is it affecting your stamina and mental clarity?
- What are your thoughts on how to gain control?

SECTION 4: ONWARD + BEYOND

Chapter 34
It's ok to Shrink

> "A woman is unstoppable after she realizes she deserves better." -Unknown

The critical piece about this book is to take action to keep moving forward. As you expand yourself and heal the conditions of your heart, you will realize very quickly that there is a rebirth happening in your life. After all the cord cutting, energy to remove blocks, and reframe of language your soul begins to revive itself and you have a BREAKTHROUGH.

When a rebirth happens, you become your true and authentic self, you begin to obtain more clarity on what is your soul purpose. This is also a tender time for yourself. Be very gentle. You will shed some tears, feel very uncomfortable at times, and question even why you are investing this energy into yourself and feel horrible at the same time. DON'T GIVE UP! Keep the momentum going strong!

Just like an athlete needs recovery time, so do you Tenacious Queen. You may need more quiet time than usual to allow the change to penetrate your soul. Give yourself a few days to recharge and recalibrate. Netflix binge, get some more pampering time with a massage, or hang out some friends for a night of dancing and fun.

You are at a stage in your life that you have become more mindful and aware of your power, shifts, and stories. You look out to your horizon and see the silver lining, a blur of your purpose and calling. It may not be all formulated or understood, but you are getting more clarity.

Remember the **rubber band analogy I shared in Section 2?** Read it again if you have to as a refresher. In order to keep expanding you have to stay tenacious on moving past every obstacle and mindset block. Even this beyond uncomfortable feeling means you are on track. The object is to keep expanding your rubber band a little more and more and more each day. When you keep pressing forward you continuously expand the rubber band. Don't be afraid of the band snapping because all that means is its time to upgrade to a larger one which means BIGGER expansion and infinite possibilities.

You're in the learning stage towards this new and improved "you" to be the tenacious queen God has called you to be. You'll for a moment forget about your power and begin to revert back to old habits and patterns. When things get uncomfortable, our first instinct is to run away from the pain. This is when it's time to make a fight or flight decision. Typically, our first instinct were to run away from the pain. You'll get out of balance. You will feel very constricted at the beginning then you will be reminded to step into the bigger size version of "You" which is way easier than before; your expansion will become fuller and fuller. The more you expand the more room you have to achieve your dreams.

You may even start sabotaging yourself. Increasing your tenacity can be unsettling at the beginning; your new power and endurance can be terrifying. This uncomfortable feeling will make you feel a bit out of control to the point of wanting to abort the process. I promise its ok to feel like this. I promise it will get easier. This new mindset can play games on your conscious thoughts. Your breakthrough is not false, it's just simply "new". Remember our brains can become fearful of even successful thoughts.

But when we lean into discomfort, and let ourselves soften, it's almost like we're gifted with a whole new perspective and new stamina to proceed. Life can be the most amazing teacher; it offers the most profound lessons at the right times. When we are overwhelmed with emotional feelings such as sadness, confusion, jealousy, frustration, or anger, then life is offering an opportunity to expand or upgrade your rubber band to understand where you're stuck in your growth, where you have more to learn, where you could focus your attention.

Leaning into emotions allow us to explore the feelings, consider the lessons we can learn from the situation. When something makes you uncomfortable — whether it's as simple as a rude comment from a family member or as life altering as losing a source of income in your home or a devastating illness — we develop a narrative about what we've just experienced. We'll go through a phase of feeling insulted, betrayed, hurt. Then we may even convince ourselves of why this unpleasant thing has happened which eventually impacts our self-worth. "They don't respect me," for example, transforms into, "I'm not worthy of respect." "He doesn't love me," can become, "I'm not lovable." After we lean into the emotions and analyze the feelings we can come to understand that the "uncomfortable" feeling which was once our enemy or the worst-case scenario in our minds, becomes the ally to greater personal growth and development to be an unstoppable Queen.

Time to Slay:

- In what ways, do you feel uncomfortable?

- How can you lean into the discomfort on your journey?

- Repeat to yourself right now, "This is new and this awesome"! Say it with power! This is not an overnight process. You may experience these thoughts back and forth for days, weeks, or even months depending on how much you are reconfiguring your "mental operating system".

Chapter 35
Be an Unstoppable Queen

> "I choose to be unstoppable. I am bigger than my concerns and worries. The strength of others inspires me daily. I focus on my goal. I trust my intuition and live a courageous life." - Unknown

My deceased step father had a friend who couldn't stand my guts. I am so serious. This man didn't like me and honestly, I didn't like him either. We had a mutual relationship. He said I had a bad attitude and always had something smart to say. I do agree with him. Yes, I had my opinions and would freely share them when I felt the urge. That darn chip on my shoulder from the abuse I had experienced as a child made me feel so annoyed and betrayed by all men. This man hated me so much that he called me "Eric" instead of "Erica".

He even said it with an attitude without enunciating the "r" in the word. Even the way he looked at me was off putting, as if he was so disgusted with me. One day he came over to our house, displaying tension with me in his usual manner. He said he was going to get my sister ice cream, but not get me any because he claimed I had an attitude with him when he arrived. He returned with a vanilla ice cream cone for my younger sister. Her face lit up so bright with excitement and joy.

Also, like any other 5-year-old sibling, my sister teased me since I didn't have my own ice cream. This is exactly what he wanted. I said, "ok" with spunk, sass, and foot stomping as I walked away. I disappeared for a short period of time. No one to this day know where I went (including myself). When I returned, I came back with my own ice cream. Everyone looked at me in astonishment. I could see my mom have a small smirk on her face as if she wanted to laugh. They truly couldn't believe I did this. I licked that cone so hard and with the most sass I could display with my eyes and expression. I do remember locking eyes with the friend of the family for a moment as I ate my ice cream.

He was little embarrassed looking at me like a dog does when you walk into the house after they know they did something wrong and can't make direct contact. I wish God would show me what I did to get my ice cream. I didn't have money and I hope I didn't steal it or hurt someone for it. But the moral of this story is that I didn't let this man tell me I couldn't partake in something good. I felt like I was entitled to enjoy some good ole ice cream. This is how we need to be with our goals. We have to make a way out of no way. We have to be our own saving grace.

You have to be 100% dedicated to your dreams. The dreams are free, but the hustle is sold separately. This required thinking forces us to go out of the box and against the grain sometimes. You will not make everyone happy. Everyone will not be in your corner cheering for you. Sometimes that dream will disconnect you from people. You have to stay focused on your goal and your vision. Never let ANYONE including yourself dull your dream or your plans. You take those concerns to God and allow him to console you and provide more insight on the next steps to take.

> "The devil doesn't know what to do with somebody who just won't give up." –Joyce Myers

Time to Slay:

- How can you be an unstoppable Queen with your goals?

- What/Who is in your way of your dreams? How can you shift things to make room for your desires?

- What excuses have you been using lately which is preventing you from taking the steps necessary to live the life you have always dreamed of?

Chapter 36

Queen Rituals (Consistency is Key)

> "A Queen on her throne is a woman who has mastered herself. She's not perfect, but she is complete. She has come to full realization that everything she needs to fulfill her mission can be found within. She uncovered her powers and she knows how to use them. She's no longer on the path, she has become the path." -Molesey Crawford

Consistency is the key to success in many aspects of life because success is the sum of small efforts repeated day in and day out. As a Queen, your consistent behavior shows God you mean business about your dreams and aspirations. You should make sure your behavior matches your desires. If you are seeking to be a millionaire in the future, then you should be adopting the behavioral patterns as a person who lives at that standard starting with your daily rituals and habits.

If you are seeking to be a world-renowned key note speaker you should be working on managing your schedule and calendar now so that when it fills up, you are ready and have all of the details worked out to transition into your new life with ease and grace. Consistency in daily habits and rituals serves as a model for how serious you are about achieving your dreams. If you treat your current life as unimportant, don't be surprised if you don't see your desires manifest.

Here are some great ideas on rituals you start adopting in your day-to-day life to up level your life in many ways.

Time to Slay:

1. Set Morning and Evening Intentions.
Every morning, Benjamin Franklin asked himself, "What good will I do today?" Then at night before bed he asked,

"What good did I do today?"

This is a very simple ritual, it has so much power to and if you research you will see the enormous amount of impact he made on a daily basis.

Think about the major shifts that could happen in your life if you took a minute before getting out of bed to ask yourself, "How do I intend to serve today?" Then as you're winding down in the evening ask yourself, "In what ways did I make impact?" I challenge you to do it for 30 days and be prepared to be surprised by the results. Share your results on social media using #unstoppabletenacity or in our FB group: Tenacious Queens Unite.

2. Time of Silence.
How much time do you take for yourself each day? More than likely you are not getting enough, most of us can barely get 30 secs of silence. You are more than likely waking up to kids, spouse, social media, or even straight to emails. Oprah takes 20 mins to ground herself before tackling her day. For the next 30 days' work on getting at least 10 minutes of silence by doing one of the following:

- <u>Meditate</u>-A few minutes of practice per day can help ease anxiety.

  It's simple. Sit up straight with both feet on the floor. Close your eyes. Focus your attention on reciting -- out loud or silently -- a positive mantra such as "I feel at peace" or "I love myself." Place one hand on your belly to sync the mantra with your breaths. Let any distracting thoughts float by like clouds.

- <u>Breathe Deeply</u>- Take a 5-minute break and focus on your breathing. Sit up straight, eyes closed, with a hand on your belly. Slowly inhale through your nose, feeling the breath start in your abdomen and work its way to the top of your head. Reverse the process as you exhale through your mouth. "Deep breathing counters the effects of stress by slowing the heart rate and lowering blood pressure".

3. **Performance counts**. Before every serve, Serena Williams bounces the ball exactly five times. This may sound crazy for the top tennis player to partake in each day. However, it's all about focus. When you have to perform at your best, you need to be fully present, not worried about what others will think or if you're going to blow it.

When I have to perform my best during a presentation or coaching call, I place my hand over my heart for about 3 seconds and take a deep breath to tune into my subconscious self which helps calm my spirit and clear my mind.

4. Pay if Forward. Who hasn't witnessed the power of paying it forward and giving? There is no need to wait until you achieve your ultimate dreams, you can be a giver now. Find ways to donate your time, energy, and expertise to others on a regular basis. The most successful people find a way to give on a daily basis. You never know how you can radically change someone's life and partake in the transformational process of another person. Do it without expecting anything in return.

5. Take Care of your Body

- Tune Into Your Body-Mentally scan your body to get a sense of how stress affects it each day. Lie on your back, or sit with your feet on the floor. Start at your toes and work your way up to your scalp, noticing how your body feels. Do this during your 10minutes of silence each day.

- Get Adequate Sleep- Queens we need REST! YES, good rest... not halfway or only a few hours each night. We have to start taking care of our bodies. Our temple is precious and if we slack on this simple principle, it can affect us 10 years or beyond! Regular and restful sleep is essential for good health. Sleep helps you feel less stressed and even helps you to maintain a healthy diet. Sleep deprivation can affect important aspects of your mind and body such as your mood, energy, ability to learn, memory, good judgment, reaction time and efficiency. Are you having trouble sleeping at night? Is your mind wandering?

If your mind is wandering, try a brain dumping technique: Keep a notebook and pen next to bed and if you notice your mind going and going, begin to write out those thoughts. You will be surprised what this little action does. Our mind constantly protects us; this means when you have a thought and didn't address it will replay over and over again until you either dump it or take action based on concern.

Stop using all technology 30 min before bed - no cell phone, no lap top, no kindle, NO FACEBOOK. The light blocks melatonin which can help you fall asleep. A 30-min wind down with relaxation and reading (a paper book) can make it easier to fall asleep. No caffeine after 3 PM.

Sleep only an hour longer during the weekend than your latest weekday wake-up time.

Take a nice hot bath

Avoid Soul Shattering buzzard in A.M. Instead create a soothing alarm which makes you feel great at the beginning of your day.

- Get Regular Exercise -To keep your energy levels up getting some type of exercise at minimal 3 times a week (10-20mins burst High interval training) can be very beneficial.

Chapter 37

Managing Change

> **Resilience is a reflex, a way of facing and understanding the world that is deeply etched into a person's mind and soul. Resilient people face reality with staunchness, make meaning of hardship instead of crying out in despair, and improvise solutions from thin air. Others do not.**
> **–Diane Coutu**

In 2003, I was introduced to the banking field by a friend who I attended the same church in Tacoma, Washington. My first role as a Teller was fun and exciting. I felt alive and purposeful. I was good at what I did; every customer would tell me, "I love your energy and smile!" In my mind, I knew this was what I wanted to do for a very long time. I started off with a small bank on McChord Air Force Base. Working with Airmen was very interesting, the 1st and 15th paydays were our busiest days. We did so many withdrawals to issue money orders and cashier checks or transfers to other accounts so that they could spend their cash on other obligations. There were so many over-drawn accounts and $0 account balances; it was the reality of how low military pay can be at the beginning stages until you promote. I quickly became great friends with another military wife & co-worker; we joked all day in-between customers, we even took lunch breaks together at times to discuss our personal life. We had the best times at work and she was a motivating factor to show up each and every day.

She learned that we were getting drastically underpaid compared to Tellers at a military credit union and she started the application process. She quickly left me and was making $3 more an hour. So of course, I was very intrigued since Josh and I were living on kibbles and bits with Airman 1st Class (A1C) military pay. She encouraged me to apply and said she would put in a good word for me. I interviewed and got the position. We were both very happy to be working together and thriving in our roles. We both quickly promoted to Financial Service Representatives. These are the staff who sits at the desk to serve customers with opening accounts, applying for loans, or other account transactions outside the teller scope of practice.

It was like we completely followed each other on this banking path and excelled together. Another year passed, and my friend once again learned that another bank was hiring, this time it was a nationwide bank opportunity to have more exposure and more income. The application for this bank took a little longer and required more interviews (three to be exact). She was hired first and then I was hired a few weeks after. It's so interesting that we both started off in 2003 at a small military bank as Tellers making $8 per hour and then moved up to $15 per hour at a larger more established nationwide bank. We had doubled our income within a year and half and had the potential to earn bonus checks. Unfortunately, we were not at the same locations this time around. To everything there is a season of transition and it was time for me to spread my own wings.

My boss loved me, I was the go-getter and ambitious person on the team willing to do what it took to hit our quota. I met with customers at events, talked to them in the lobby, and closed all types of sales using my gift of gab. I was the person at the end of month with the highest sales and bonuses each month. My friend and I both finished as the top 15% percentile Personal Bankers in the district and were recognized at a banquet. My friend whom I worked with before was also recognized. We immediately hugged each other to congratulate our accomplishments. There was money to be made in the Personal Banking world during that time, I remember one of my highest bonus checks being $1800 for a single month on top of salary. I felt great and honestly felt like I made a huge accomplishment. My boss loved me so much that he offered me a role in 2006 to become the Business Banker for our location which will be paying me $43,680 as a base salary and awesome bonus opportunity. I immediately accepted. But of course, there were some people on the team who were not happy with this accomplishment. I wasn't aware that a fellow colleague wanted the role. My boss loved me, but the co-worker felt like it was some favoritism in play.

After about a week, Human resources was involved in my promotion and were claiming it was invalid due to my short tenure with the company. In addition, they claimed that I was closing sales inappropriately; my boss said I could fight the claims, but instead I left the company because I felt very uncomfortable and betrayed to have such a horrible reputation to battle. At the same time, Joshua was being faced with a decision at the end of his first 4-year term in active duty military. He was very discouraged that his dream job which was promised from initial enlistment as a Visual Information Technician was phasing out of the military.

He was presented two choices: to get out of active duty or they will choose his next Air Force specialty code. We were both left with no jobs at this point in Washington State. We were lost on what to do next. A friend from our church invited us to stay at her home for a short period of time until we decide on our next step. We decided to move into an apartment and signed a 1 year lease. We were in the apartment for about 3 months and decided to move back home (Cleveland, Ohio). In a matter of 4 months, our life changed drastically.

As you can see, my husband and I are masters of change. It gets better. Can you believe we have lived in 11 places in the last 14 years of marriage? Yes, it's the God honest truth, we have moved so many times that we have it down to a science and know how to move with no assistance from others. Our moves were associated with military, corporate relocations, and personal choices. There were times when Josh would put a full-sized sofa on his back to move it from one place to another. We are the "OCD" movers who has all their boxes perfectly labeled and organized to the max so that when we unload our goods they can be put away with ease. In addition, we would perfectly stack boxes on top of each other and secure with shrink wrap to use the dolly to move up to 5 boxes all at the same time. We are efficient movers! Now, don't think about asking us to help you move though, we are not professional movers to others, just ourselves. We will make sure we are busy when you are looking for help during your next move.

As we reflect, we can't even believe the changes and transitions we have successfully conquered. We recognize that most other couples could not handle the life we have experienced up until now. Our move in 2009 was devastating and frustrating; we were in the process of buying this beautiful new home in the Westpark area of Cleveland, Ohio. It was a rent-to-own home and they were helping us with our credit the whole time while we resided there to make sure we would be approved for final bank loan. We were renting there for about 18 months and just knew we were going to buy it. However, we made a very dumb child-like decision to go on a cruise and blow thousands of dollars instead of paying off a few old credit cards they instructed us to do to ensure we got final approval to buy the house. In our defense, we had gone through many circles with this financial company for 18 long months on attempts to get us approved and we began to get tired and just needed a break from the usual atmosphere.

In addition, right before my eyes in broad day light (11am) I had witnessed two trespassers forcefully entered our neighbor's home to steal all her electronics. I immediately called the police, but when they arrived they were already gone. For several weeks after incident, I was scared when Josh went to work. I was afraid of them returning to our home thinking someone wasn't present. We felt unsafe and doubting if we really wanted to stay in the neighborhood.

So, we went on vacation to let our hair down a bit and relax. Then when we returned from the cruise our financial counselor told us that they were still having problems getting us approved for the loan and would have to raise the rent $300/month to extend our contract. Josh had just completed his 9-month full-time military contract in Youngtown, Ohio which was our main source of income while I pursued my educational goals. The thought of paying $300 more a month seemed impossible for us at that time. We decided to move in with my mom, step-father, and sister. During this period of time, we had already been married for 6 years, so you can only imagine the embarrassment and frustration we were feeling thinking to ourselves, "Oh Lord, we are moving back in with parents."

Our energy was very low and we were not excited about the decision. However, we felt like it was needed to get back on track and come up with a better game plan for our life, it was just tough to embrace this transition with open arms. As we packed for this move, we didn't have the music blasting as we normally do or fully participated in our OCD moving procedures since everything was going into storage. We had laser focus; there was no room for fun and games. We were focused on all work, no play.

There was so much uncertainty to how this would work out and all we could do was stay focused on getting all of our items loaded and then unloaded into the storage unit. As we loaded the 20ft moving truck, we griped and complained the whole time with one another and about life in general. We further determined we didn't have enough room for all of our stuff on the truck and should have rented the 26ft truck for the number of items we had in the house. We ended up doing two trips to transfer everything into storage.

To add to our frustration, Josh accidently hit a car tucked into his blind spot as he made a wide right-hand turn on the corner of W. 105th and Lorain in Cleveland, Ohio. The person immediately jumped out of the car and pulled a gun out on us. Talk about a horrible transition into change. We both put our hands up and pleaded with him in fear that we didn't see him. We were not only frustrated about moving, but now we were scared for our lives. We eventually got the man to calm down to have a real conversation with us to exchange insurance information. When we arrived at Mama May's house that evening we were physically, mentally, and spiritually drained. Can you relate, have you been here before?

We live in a world of constant change. India Arie sings in her song "Growth": the only thing constant in the world is change/that's why today I take life as it come. Nature is an example of constant birth, growth, death, and renewal. Understanding the cycles of life will help us thrive in change, rather than dread it. Life would be quite boring if we encountered the same old scenarios, threats and challenges; they would lose the opportunity to help us expand our "rubber band". But when we're confronted with the unfamiliar, the unthinkable, the unimaginable, we have nothing to fall back on and are forced to creatively cope with the transition. While transitions such as those crazy moves my husband and I experienced can be painful and uncertain, they are a segment to develop more creativity, growth and transformation.

My clients come to me seeking creative ways to cope, maximize, and resolve their life or business circumstances. And the first thing I help them do is help them undergo a psychological transition to cultivate resilience which can proceed with a sense of adventure. This is the most important resource during times of crisis, change and transition. Change is situational; a new job, new home, new business all require transitional periods. From a psychological perspective, coping with transitions are the most difficult aspects to handle when change appears in our life, says William Bridges, author of *Managing Transitions*.

Here are 4 ways to thrive during times of transition:

1. Develop a Sense of Optimism

Resilient people face difficult situations realistically, yet find ways to be optimistic. Studies indicate optimists live longer, have better relationships, and achieve more success in life. Optimists are not magical thinkers, unable to see the tough side of the coin; rather, they embrace reality, and immediately put things in perspective.

2. Dig Deep to Find the Meaning in Unsettling Times

Eckhart Tolle explains in *The Power of Now* offers profound lessons on being conscious of the present moment in every situation, especially dire situations. He further explains that meaning and purpose is found in every moment of living; life never ceases to have meaning, even in suffering and death. "Stress is caused by being 'here' but wanting to be 'there'. No matter what is going on, you can always choose your attitude, and show up, by setting an example for others."

3. Stand in your Power

In times of turbulence, it's helpful to focus on what is truly in our power to control. As Albert Einstein wisely said: "Out of clutter, find Simplicity. From discord, find Harmony. In the middle of difficulty lies Opportunity."

4. Master your Creativity Skills

> "When life gives you lemons...make lemonade, lemon meringue pie, lemon cupcakes, and lemon rum iced drinks."- Erica Stepteau

Resilient people are masters of innovation and resourcefulness. They have the capacity to improvise and are masters at using a variety of materials that happen to be available.

Creative expression has the power to heal emotions, and nurture the soul. When we enter the flow states of complete absorption in a creative process, we open our awareness to new perceptions, and new perspectives. Creativity is something you can control. When you take time to create, you shift your field of attention into something generative and life affirming.

Time to Slay:

- How can you embrace change more in your life? In what ways, can you maximize the experience?
- How could you improvise at home or at work? What resources do you have available to you, to utilize in new ways?
- Which one of the tips above do you need the most help with? How will you start shifting your mindset and or actions to relinquish control?

Chapter 38
Dealing with Uncertainty

> "When you are going through a difficult situation and wonder where God is, remember that the teacher is always quiet during the test." –Unknown

Money and *Uncertainty* were two words that sent me into an emotional imbalance and when you put those two words together for my situation it would put me into depression. I couldn't stand not knowing when and where my money was coming from that is why for a few years, I had a very hard time dealing with entrepreneurial efforts. I needed a paycheck for a specific salary amount on a specific date to have inner peace. This would disturb every aspect of my being. I had to learn to lean into the uncomfortable feeling and also embrace unclear pockets of life with open arms and excitement. When I started mastering how I responded to job losses, unexpected bills, and inconsistent client payments that is when I began to evolve to another level in my journey.

Recently my husband lost his job due to budget cuts, they told him at 3pm on a Wednesday that it was his last day, but that they would pay him through Friday. This was a week before Christmas and during the prep to launch this book. I still had some financial obligations to purchase books for the launch party, Unstoppable Tenacity shirts that I already committed to prior to the news, and the cost of the launch party itself. Normally something like this would send me into frustration, worry, and full blown anxiety. Instead, I graciously accepted the opportunity and kept focused on this project to finish this book for all of lives which would transform with these words as they read them. I knew this book had a higher purpose to touch millions of lives and I had to trust that God would supply all of my needs. I know I passed that test with flying colors for the first-time in my adult life! I didn't freak out about uncertain income and didn't become upset about "why" it was happening to me. It was refreshing to let it roll off my shoulders and fully trust the process. In addition, it was rewarding to know that I had expanded into a new rubber band on my journey. You can do it as well and I will show you how.

You've probably heard some version of the phrase: The only thing certain in life is uncertainty. The fact that life is filled with surprises, unexpected events and change – a whole lot of it – it's not necessarily a bad thing. It's simply reality. This is how life works. And every opportunity helps us grow stronger with each test.

Unfortunately, for many of us uncertainty can be quite uncomfortable. It's especially tough tolerating uncertainty when a situation is significant to us, and we become attached to a specific outcome, according to Brene Brown.

For instance, you might be uncomfortable with uncertainty when a relationship is experiencing a rough patch or when there's a chance your job is being eliminated due to budget cuts. Because uncertainty is distressing, many of us try to control or eliminate it altogether. I regularly see this with my clients who struggle with anxiety. When we lose total control, anxiety comes to surface.

Furthermore, I have witnessed many entrepreneurs become more and more frustrated on their journey when they do everything that another entrepreneur has done to accomplish a specific success such as a 5-figure launch or acquire a new client. However, after following all of the steps, the success in their head does not match their reality. They do not understand how it worked for "Jane Doe" and not work for them. They become anxious and start doing everything they can think of to make it happen. Or another example is a woman attempting to lose weight and she has been juicing for months and working out like a mad woman, but the number on the scale has not budged one pound. She no longer feels like she is in control and therefore her frustrations increase to the point she either gives up completely on her goal or loses hope in the dream.

I would like to provide you some tips on how to effectively deal with uncertainty. Because let's face it, there are many times in our lives which we won't have 100% control over and it's important to understand our role in the manner so that we maximize our time and energy appropriately. As we master this behavior, we will energetically release the need to feel like we have to control every aspect of our lives and be in peace with normal aspects of the human experience to continually evolve as a Tenacious Queen.

> **"Life challenges and periods of uncertainty are normal aspects of the human experience...They promote the evolution of our consciousness."**
> **-Joyce Marter**

Time to Slay:

Let Go of Outcome:
"If we go through life attached to the idea that things 'should' or 'must' go a certain way, we set ourselves up for endless disappointment," said Corboy, co-author of The Mindfulness Workbook for OCD. *How can you loosen your grip on how things should be? Can you be open to other possibilities or outcomes?*

Manage Anxious Thoughts
Cognitive restructuring is a core of Cognitive Behavioral Therapy which is a powerful way to get more comfortable with uncertainty. Basically, you no longer accept the automatic negative thought which come so easily to your mind, instead you challenge those thoughts said Corboy. For example, when the thought arises in mindset saying, "I can't handle uncertainty about loss of my husband job", replace it with "I don't particularly care for uncertainty with my money, but I can bear it and I know God has my back." *What thoughts associated with uncertainty do you need to replace? Give it a try and place in your Unstoppable Tenacity journal.*

Let God Handle the Details
Your focused intentions set the infinite organizing power of the universe in motion. Trust that God has your back and knows your desires. At times, you have to silence the voice that says that you have to

be in charge with obsessive efforts because it's the only way to get anything done. Forcing things to happen is not the same as it naturally and organically formulating. You have released your intentions into the fertile ground of pure potentiality which will bloom when the season is right.

REST > RELEASE > REMAIN

Rest in "The Gap"

Most of the time our mind is caught up in thoughts, emotions, and memories. Beyond this noisy internal dialogue and gremlins speaking loud is a state of pure awareness that is sometimes referred to as "the gap." One of the most effective tools we have for entering the gap is through meditation. Meditation help takes you beyond the ego-mind into the silence and stillness of our subconscious mind. This is the ideal state in which to plant your seeds of intention and gain strength in clarity.

Release Your Intentions and Desires Once you rest in the "the gap" and gain maximum restful awareness then it's time to release your intentions and desires. The best time to plant your intentions is during the period after meditation, while your awareness remains centered in the quiet field of all infinite possibilities. After you set an intention, release them to God to handle it —simply stop thinking about it. Continue this process for a few minutes after your meditation period each day.

Remain Centered in a State of Restful Awareness

Intention is much more powerful when it comes from a place of contentment than if it arises from a sense of lack or need. Stay centered and refuse to be influenced by other people's doubts or criticisms. People will not understand your grind nor your dreams. It's not for them to understand. Trust that your higher self-intuition knows everything will be all right, even without knowing all of the details of what will happen.

Chapter 39
Manage your Energy

> "If you want to be more productive, you need to become master of your minutes." –Crystal Paine

As tenacious queens, we manage multiple tasks in a day and may feel like we have to divide our attention. We experience MANY distractions (even the self-imposed distractions) which lead to lapses in concentration, poor results and less fulfillment. I remember there was a time in my business when I was working 14-16 hrs. a day. All online in pajamas on the computer. I was determined to interact with prospective clients, stay visible, and analyze my competition. My mindset and type-A efforts were just putting me in circles and leaving me very aggravated and broke. I realized very quickly this was so beyond dangerous for my health and slashing into the luxury of "time freedom" which I thought I would have by working as an online entrepreneur. It took me a few months to catch on to the bad habits and priorities I set in my life during that timeframe.

When you work that hard you actually constrict your capacity to receive. Just think the type of slave mentality a person may have when they feel like they have to work, work, work. Yes, I know you just thought about Rhianna's song. She tainted us with that song. Why does our society think working MORE, working HARDER, and working LONGER deems a person as successful?

It's the exact opposite! You are unsuccessful. Why? Because you don't have time to have fun, you don't have time to spend the money you are making, you barely have evening slots opened to be social, and your weekends are crammed with errands and chores. Sounds like a rat race to me.

When I began to manage my energy appropriately it created more abundant thoughts and signals to the universe to continue to bless me. I actually managed to hit my first 5 figure month in biz without working 14-16 days. It was more like 7-8 hours days. I worked less than I did as a full-time employee and made double the profit. Working harder and longer isn't the answer. It all comes down to energy, focus and intentionality.

I want to help you discover ways to get more balance. You don't need a spa weekend or a retreat. It starts with understanding the difference between busyness and productivity. In your list of ongoing tasks and agendas, a word may come up which will reveal to you if you are managing your energy appropriately. Let's talk about that "B" word: (Busy). Here's a great question to pounder as you juggle multiple roles every day: "**Are you Busy or Are You Productive?**"

We need to know the difference between the two. We can be "Busy" all day long and accomplish NOTHING or we can be Productive to accomplish so much more. All because you sit at a computer all day/run around like a chicken with its head cut off doesn't mean you are effectively getting things done.

Peter Drucker, who has written more than 30 books including, "The Practice of Management", in which Drucker developed "Management by Objectives" (MBO), a management concept based on objective-setting and self-supervision, said: "What gets measured gets managed." Unfortunately, most people believe being busy means they are getting things done, but this is often not the case. Ladies it's time to organize our lives and measure our success!

Here are 3 keys ways to manage your minutes in your day to create more productivity:

1. **Know when to say "No"**
2. **Know when to invest your time**
3. **Organize your life in a way that encourages strategy with ease and flow.**

Time to Slay:

- How are you managing your energy?
- Everyday write down 3 tasks you want to accomplish with no distractions (3 laser focus intentions).
- Then write down what needs to be done to fulfill those intentions. This should help you ensure that you are not in circles. It also requires a bit of upfront planning which is the key to success! Check back to your list on an intention list at midday. At end of day check list to measure what was accomplished and what you weren't able to tackle.
- REPEAT each and every day. To take to another level find an accountability partner! This tool is VERY helpful in making sure you are not just

    "Busy" but Productive!!

Chapter 40
Shutdown the Comparison

> "Be confident. Too many days are wasted comparing ourselves to others and wishing to be something we aren't. Everybody has their own strengths and weaknesses, and it is only when you accept, everything you are and everything you aren't that you will truly succeed in life."
> – Ritu Ghatourey

After taking a 1 year entrepreneurial break due to emotional and family issues, I began to step in the realm of "self-judgment" when I returned and saw entrepreneurs who stayed consistent and up-leveled to many different opportunities and basically left me in the dust. It really stabbed me in the heart when I saw an online coach who basically started when I launched my Weight Management Coaching Program and she was on track to make 7-figures that year. She was killing it with every post, her following grew from 3k to 12k and was beginning to reap the benefits of her consistent dedication. I wasn't infatuated about the money, it was the dream of freedom, endless opportunities, and impact she was encountering each and every day.

I instantly started condemning myself for taking a step back in my business. Thinking, "wow, Erica you really suck at being consistent, you give up so quickly; I bet the outpouring of blessings you were seeking were right at your fingertips, but you gave up." So much sadness entered my mindset at that moment. Thinking *how in the hell will I get my business back in full motion*? I had a huge following at some point, discovery calls every single day and even hit a few 5-figures months as a full-time entrepreneur. Our society are comparison junkies and the fact is comparison is truly a natural tendency. From the start of birth, new born babies are openly or secretly compared to each other to see who is smarter, cuter, or even more alert. Then when children begin their school-age years, games are played to see how one can answer the questions the fastest, win the most stickers on the board, or win other achievements. Which cause children to compare what they won or didn't win and analyze how fast someone is able to learn vs. how slow some learn. Brene Brown shares that, "comparing yourself to others can preclude a bond of common fellowship and is a disservice to finding true worth. No one is above anyone else. Self-esteem must come from simply being you."

What someone else achieved will be a bit different from you. People get discouraged when they can't lose a certain amount of weight in the same time frame as someone else. It's okay since every person's body is designed differently. Likewise, your journey is completely differently than another person. Letting go of comparison requires self-compassion rather than beating yourself up, you will praise yourself and gain a higher level of self-esteem from your efforts to deal with jealousy or envy positively. The end result will foster a loving spirit versus defensive posture in relationships. It can be absolutely neutral, as when you merely evaluate similarities and differences.

Comparing ourselves to others derives from low self-esteem and lack of belief in the integrity of our own unique character or life path. In simple terms, comparing our path to another is similar to comparing apples and pears. Why? Our lives are explicitly designed for our own personal growth journey. Every person we meet, every situation we encounter, every challenge we face help us become a stronger, more compassionate, and wiser person. It's imperative to appreciate the grace of both the hurdles and the joys of this thing we call "life". This is the ultimate purpose and legacy for each and every one of us to experience. Self-esteem comes from embracing this, working with what each day brings. How you spend your time here is up to you. Why dilute it by comparing? Realistically, we will still do it because it's natural to compare. Regardless, let's strive to keep our eyes on ourselves to build self-esteem so we can become more unstoppable in our efforts towards our dreams.

Now when I look at all the women who have achieved some major goals in their online businesses or overcame major obstacles I no longer get jealous or doubt I could do what they have done. If the doubt gremlins and resistance gremlins comes into my mind I instantly start asking myself the following questions: *Why can I not have what they have? How are they different than me? What makes them so special?* When you start answering these questions you will quickly see that these people are not much smarter, special, or even more gifted than you. Now of course I have had my fair share of jealousy and comparison, especially in the business arena. I watched women killing it in their online businesses and wondering what I was doing wrong. Why do I feel like I don't have the following or tribe as they do? Why can I not have $100K launches and daily passive income? As soon as I focused on those questions I began to shrink my capacity to receive and a ton of resistance starts to build back up all over again. It's imperative for myself to keep my mind in check at all times.

My tenacity (continual self -improvement) kicks in and I reframe those thoughts back to confidence building thoughts. I also learned I had to let go of the focus around stats and figures and open up my mindset to the transformation and authentic connection with my tribe. I was prompted to start a group called "Tenacious Queens Unite" on Facebook. This group is all about me being the most authentic and raw I have ever been on my journey. This all sparked from a very powerful presentation by Lisa Nichols. She explained that "your story is your fuel" and "your success is in your dips". I downloaded the most moving vision and insight from that phrase. It all hit me at that moment: all the pain, heartaches, confusion, and losses were all aligned and purposeful for me to share with women to empower them to rise up and claim their unstoppable power towards the life they dream to achieve. Now I am on a daily mission to do just that via this book, conferences, online courses, and group coaching.

> **"Where you are, is just fine. You can get to where you are. It's time to stop measuring where you are in relationship to where anybody else it. The only factor that has anything to do with you is where you are in relationship with where you want to be."**
>
> **- Abraham Hicks**

Time to Slay:

Below I would like for you to try the following exercises I have helped my clients adopt in their journey to turn jealousy and envy around. The more you practice it, the easier it will get.

> Choose the person you find yourself a little jealous or envious of. It's ok to admit this, this is the only way you can truly move forward. This person can be a friend, co-worker, fellow entrepreneur, or even a family member. Use this person as the test case to help you to apply the steps below and start the transformational process of letting go of comparison and healing jealously within your heart.
>
> Enlisting the methods below will help you take your eyes off of others' journey and back to yourself. It will force you to appreciate what you have rather than focus on what you're lacking.
>
> - **Try a Different Approach**: Practice dealing with jealousy and envy by mindfully using humility even if the person irritates or bother you. For example, rather than allowing your emotions rise when this person gets praised for something great. Instead second the awesome achievement of him or her as an act of empowerment for yourself. Send them your blessings. Even if it's hard to do this, try. It helps you to turn negativity around to something more positive. Prior to your act of service and acknowledgement for this practice the

affirmation, "I will not compare". Then shift your mindset to start focusing on something you do have and what makes you happy about yourself. This will shift your mindset and become the tone of the conversation.

- **Give to others what you most desire for yourself**. If you want to be recognized, recognize others. If you want more compassion, give compassion. If you want a successful business, help another entrepreneur flourish in their business. Karma is something else. What goes around comes around, this can be an energetic dynamic you can mobilize.

- **Understand Their Prospective**. Get your mind off of what you perceive you lack and towards improving yourself on the path. Yoko Ono says, "Transform jealousy to admiration, and what you admire will become part of your life," this is an incredible message to live by. Once you understand their perspective and what has been their unique path, you become more inspired than jealous.

Chapter 41

Ruffle the Feathers & Speak your Truth

> "If feathers don't ruffle, nothing flies."
> - Jessica Raine

Tenacity will affect your relationship with others and force you to ruffle the feathers of those around you. When I started attending church at the age of 13 years old, my mom wasn't the biggest fan. When I reflect back, I see how she may have felt like I spent too much time at church instead of home. I felt like I was exiled and verbally abused for making this decision.

At the same time, I know I wasn't the nicest to my mom and rubbed church into her face because I was still dealing with old emotional wounds. It was very hurtful when my mom refused to take me to church. I was sad and would cry many nights because I could not understand why she was so upset with me for doing something "right". I could have been out in the streets having sex, using drugs, or other "normal" teenage activities. All I wanted to do was be in the House of the Lord and socialize with like-minded peers instead of hanging out with the typical teenagers at my high school.

A few women at the church learned of my circumstance and offered to rotate to pick me up for Wednesday and Sunday services; I will never forget those 3 special women who offered their time and dedication in making sure I could attend services each week. I felt so supported at church. It was a place of safe refuge for me and unconditional love. I know getting those rides didn't help with my relationship with my mom at that time, but I honestly didn't know what else to do. I now see as an adult that my mom didn't know anything about these women or church. She just wanted to protect me and keep me safe from any potential harm.

Sometimes you are going to ruffle the feathers of others as a tenacious queen. Unfortunately, we live in a day and age now that questions our uniqueness and claims that a person wants to be in the spotlight if they chose to do something in a different manner. Instead of questioning why you decide to follow along with the crowd, people now question why a person veered from the norm. Thinking and doing differently has suddenly become a negative.

The Art of Non-Conformity by Chris Guillebeu summarizes this idea perfectly.

He shared that as adults there is an expectation on how you should live. "People start expecting you to behave very much like they do. It's almost as if they are asking: 'Hey, everyone else is jumping off the bridge. Why aren't you?'"

As soon as you step away from the standard way of living, you're immediately in the spotlight and it's not to recognize you in a great way. Thinking differently now has people question your decisions. Asking, "what is she up to now?", "why can't she be like the rest of us?"

I don't know about you, but I value my uniqueness and I have no problem going against the grain anymore. It doesn't always feel comfortable and it sure as heck will not make everyone feel warm and fuzzy all the time. I am not excusing disobedience of parents; but if I would had followed the orders of my mom by not attending church, then I would have never found my soul mate (my husband). I think our society desperately needs to take doing what the desire without so much concern of others to heart and know it's ok to ruffle the feathers of people around: if everyone else jumped off the bridge, would you? Have you? Are you living the life that you truly desire, or one by someone else's standard?

I encourage you to take time to step back and reflect on your own values and priorities, to decide how you want to live your life and silence the voice of others and their opinions. Decide today to live your life to your fullest desires. You do not need to live life like everyone else. Your life is far too valuable to be wasted on the life that everyone else is choosing. Most of the time ruffling the feathers of others strike their ego since you may be participating or achieving something they wish they can do or have. The way I see it is that I am helping them expand their thinking, they now see the endless possibility of acting in greatness and maybe it will spark them to give their dream or desire a shot.

Time to Slay:

- How are you emulating others in your life?
- How can you step into your own "zone of genius" and live life on your terms?
- In what ways, can you let go of what others think and be unapologetically you?

Chapter 42
Embrace the Path

> "Most humans are never fully present in the now, because unconsciously they believe that the next moment must be more important than this one. But then you miss your whole life, which is never not now. And that's a revelation for some people; to realize that your life is only ever now."
> – Eckhart Tolle

How many of you are waiting on something right now? A relationship, a new client, a financial breakthrough, a child, or specific number on the scale? Having trouble mastering patience? I think we all need additional lessons in this department. It can be hard at times when you are on a journey with uncertainty and trusting the process while not understanding how long you will be on these tracks towards your dream. I look back and there were many times I lost patience and really believe I lost momentum towards my goals and basically had to reevaluate my behavior so that I could keep the momentum and stay tenacious on my dreams.

Every Christmas my husband and I get dressed up in Christmas themed costumes and do a photoshoot to embrace the "in-between" stage of our journey towards fertility. We have done this 3 years in a row so far and it helps so much since we don't get to wake up on Christmas morning and witness kids opening gifts. For years, this was a burning pain for us, we would wake on Christmas morning and literally be really sad that we couldn't hear the joy in the air of Christmas scratching the paper off of boxes and children playing with toys all day. We both discussed previously how we have always dreamed of having kids waking us up early Christmas morning ecstatic to receive a toy they wanted all year. This feeling was especially important to Joshua since he came from a large family of 7 and they had a very rowdy Christmas morning filled with excited kids, boxes, and the noise of new toys. In comparison, our quiet/mellow Christmas mornings were a shell shock for him at the beginning of our marriage. I tried to make it fun by always cooking a large breakfast and playing Christmas songs along with my homemade peppermint hot chocolate.

This one particular Christmas morning we woke up and it was pure silence and sadness in the air. You could hear a pin drop in the room and you could feel our broken hearts shattering one layer at a time in the atmosphere as if it was shattered glass slowly expanding across the windshield of a vehicle or the agonizing gut feeling of listening to nails scratch across a black board. This day was a painful reminder that we have yet to achieve the blessing of a child in our lives. We looked at each other with little words to say because we knew what the other was feeling. We knew the questions we felt and the void in our hearts that wanted to cry out.

Unfortunately, we were both depleted and couldn't fill the tank of the other. Instead, we embraced each other in silence and cried with one another; Josh's tears slowly dripped on my left shoulder as my tears dripped on his right-hand. We held onto each other with a tight grip and released the sadness. After approximately 30 minutes, we started talking about what was going on in our minds and both came up with a conclusion on how to embrace this sad path as we consistently strive towards fertility. We decided to make the best out of it. We put Mickey (our 7-year-old rat terrier dog) in his Santa sweater, I put on my Mrs. Claus apron as an outfit, and Josh wore a Santa hat so that we could take a Christmas family photo. We had a ball taking pictures. We placed my Canon on the tri-pod with a timer and easily took over 200 pictures. We captured all types of poses and were playing with one another like little teenagers similar to how we were during the car wash all almost 20 years ago; So much flirting and laughter. This activity provided an idea for us, we thought, "hmmm, how about we do this every year and we create our own backdrops for the photoshoot and name it Annual Stepteau Family Christmas Photoshoot?" We began to plan the next year photos and strategizing the projects we will need to complete in order to pull it off.

For two years, we dressed up as Mr. and Mrs. Claus and our dog was in his Santa outfit and the third year we were all dressed as Elves and Joshua even wore peppermint striped tights. Don't worry he kept the look urban and cool at the same time; he was quite handsome. Others were impressed on how he pulled the outfit off and how creative we were. The year we were elves we were living back in Cleveland, Ohio (our home town) and were able to travel to family members' homes to show off the costumes and get even more in the Christmas spirit. Everyone was taking pictures with us as if we were stars. This brought so much joy to us and helped us completely forget the desire to watch kids open gifts on Christmas morning. We decided to fill the void instead of creating a pity party (as we did for several years prior to creating this activity).

Throughout my 13-year journey towards fertility, I've done a lot of inner work to maintain joy, peace, and an awesome connection with my husband. Infertility can assault a marriage and it is one of the toughest challenges a couple can face. Based on the National Infertility Association, 1 in 8 couples have trouble getting pregnant or sustaining pregnancy. Furthermore, a recent study proves couples are three times more likely to divorce after failed fertility treatments. I am beyond thankful for the connection my husband and I have had throughout the roller coasters.

Unfortunately, infertility was considered grounds for divorce at one point and time. According to the Center for Disease Control and Prevention, an estimated 10 percent of the population in childbearing years experiences some degree of infertility. Number of women ages 15-44 with impaired fertility (impaired ability to get pregnant or carry a baby to term): 6.7 million, according to the CDC. "Couples experiencing infertility often suffer marital discord due to stress from several sources including the financial strain of invasive high tech infertility treatments that can cost tens of thousands of dollars and have no guarantee of success; the emotional strain – shame, guilt and inadequacy – that many men and women endure as they struggle with the inability to produce biological children; and the physical strain from treatments that involve hormone and other drug therapies that can cause fatigue, nausea, headaches, mood swings, weight gain and disruption of the sleep cycle"- Resolve The National Infertility Association

In short, the frustration and resentment can grow from years of failed attempts that can lead to irreparable damage to the emotional health of a marriage, especially in the case similar to my husband and I since we have been attempting to get pregnant for more than 10 years AND suffered multiple failed pregnancies.

I really believe my husband and I are "against the grain" when it comes to these statistics because we chose to embrace the "in-between" stage instead of letting it control us on this journey. Through it all we have gotten much closer to each other, but it wasn't through magic. We had to continually work on our marriage throughout this process. We had to relinquish the rigid attachment to a specific end goal and embrace uncertainty. The attachment created fear and insecurity, while the act of detachment gave us our power back. We have to trust that everything is working out as it should and be open to endless possibilities of blessings to flood our way.

I know you may not be able to relate specifically to our fertility situation, but I want you to think about something you have been waiting on to happen in your life. Whether it's your soul mate, a financial breakthrough, healing from a severed relationship, weight loss or any other situation you feel like you don't have 100% control to make happen in your life at this moment. It so easy to get caught up and focus on the end goal and almost lose sight on the "in-between" stage.

> **"Everyone talks about the end goal, but what about the timeframe between the vision and manifestation?" – Erica Stepteau**

Don't get too caught up on the end goal. Do just enough to keep you excited about the dream without it becoming your daily obsession. It's all about balance. Remember a scarcity mindset BLOCKS blessings. As soon as you start stressing about the end goal back off until you refresh your energy.

Time to Slay:

Below are the 5 main things my husband and I constantly address to make sure we do not lose our connection and it helps us embrace the "in-between" stage to slay the impatience spirit. In addition, these same steps can help you embrace the "in-between" more on your journey regardless of your goal:

1. **Avoid Blame Game with each other**: Have you blamed a circumstance or person for the reason why you haven't achieved your dream? How can you take responsibility for where you are in your life? How can you get your power back and full control within your own heart to continuously move forward?
2. **Cultivate our relationship** (travel together/consistent date nights/ explore new hobbies): Where in your life are, you having a pity party? How can you make the best of the situation you are in? How can you think outside the box of your situation? In what ways, can you cultivate the relationship with yourself so that you are at peace with embracing process? How can you heal your pain to relinquish bitterness or frustration (refer back to Section 1: *Permission to Feel*)
3. **Keep sex spontaneous and fun**: How can you make it more fun and purposeful instead of dreading it or complaining? As you progress things will get intense and serious? How can

you conquer inpatient spirit? (refer back to Section 2: *Tap into your inner child*)
4. **Take breaks** (keep open line of communication): How can you pause more on your tenacious journey? How can you take a moment and smell the roses a bit?
5. **Get outside help when needed**: Who/What do you need for resources to make your dream a reality? Who can be the mirrors for you as you drive down the path of your dreams on a daily basis?

CONCLUSION

You have explored every facet of your life, Queen. I am very proud; you have examined your past, dove deep into your shadows, claimed your desires and it has been an honor to hold your hand through this process, but two things are true:

1. Life is messy and you might feel yanked away from your throne, but if you keep honoring your unstoppable tenacity, you will conquer this life and that throne will always be yours.

2. It is easy to charge forward with all of the principles and concepts of this book and then let them all slip away and disappear and forget your crown.

I, as a fellow Queen, command you not to. I see the greatness in you. It is time the world sees it, too.

You now see that your **power is based in the tenacity** of your **heart and you have** been reminded of your greatness as I did when I got my wake-up call to claim my throne. It's time to be the tenacious queen God has called you to be. Life is up, down, good, great and every way in-between…and it can be short. You and I have just as a good shot as anyone else at success in life because the playing field has been leveled. Anything can happen and everything is possible. A life path worth living is never straight and full of hurdles that you overcome while learning and meeting some great people who bring real joy into your life.

You have a unique opportunity in your life to make positive, valuable and long lasting contributions in your kingdom. But you have to stay off the fence of complacency and continue to take action. You have to keep moving forward in life; continue to shed emotional baggage, slay gremlins, and expand until your rubber band snaps…because you are resilient and now know how to navigate through life's challenges with ease and grace.

Today I pass to you your scepter, so that you walk graciously through your kingdom to sit on your throne with relentless visions brimming over with tenacity and intention to make major impact with yourself and with others. Remember to grab all of the bonus tools on the next page which will help you along the journey. Reflect back to the chapters as much as you need to ensure you stand in your legacy and truth.

Continue to slay with unflinching faith and relentless action.

"Always Wear your Invisible Crown."

With love,

Erica Steptean
Queen of Tenacity

BONUS TOOLS FOR TENACIOUS QUEENS

Tenacious Queen Money Journal
Start a Money Journal to explore your relationship with money, added value, and outgoing expenses. This tool will for accelerate your manifestations efforts.
www.unstoppabletenacity.com

Dream Sheet
This sheet will help paint a very clear vivid picture on how you want to live. Use the sheet to keep your thoughts organized and concise.
www.unstoppabletenacity.com

Oprah's Virtual Vision Board www.dreamitalive.com

Royalty Goals Template www.unstoppabletenacity.com

Unstoppable Tenacity 7 Week Experience
www.unstoppabletenacity.com/7weekexperience

Make sure you are following me on social media for **FREE** daily inspiration to keep the momentum to be unstoppable!

Facebook: www.facebook.com/unstoppabletenacity
Facebook Group: Tenacious Queens Unite
Instagram: erica_stepteau

Make sure you take a picture with Unstoppable Tenacity and tag me on Facebook using #unstoppabletenacity!

ACKNOWLEGEMENTS

I would like to express my gratitude to my mother. This book would not be possible if my mom didn't give birth to me. I've come from a long line of tenacious women. The women in my family has worked extremely hard in their lifetime raising kids from paycheck to paycheck and overcoming many traumatic trials. I witnessed my mom overcome several life-threatening life events. I appreciate her tenacity as she worked over 50hrs a week to bring home a little over $200 to take care of my sister and I. My mom tenaciously broke her crack cocaine addiction to obtain full custody of me after the court ordered rights to my aunt. That is true love and I will never forget that I was the motivating factor for her to get her life together. She further inspires me as she takes care of my brother, a 12year-old non-verbal epileptic & autistic child whose father died of cancer a few years ago. She continuously presses forward with little complaints and places full trust in God to provide strength and courage to her on a daily basis.

I am beyond thankful for my husband's unconditional love and support through every trial and mission we have encountered together. Joshua is my rock, best friend, lover, and soul mate. He is my #1 fan and biggest supporter. He was the person helping me with stories to include in the manuscript and supported my dream from the time it was inspired to write it (Sept 2016). He was the person who consoled me when I was frustrated, kept me laughing when I needed a break, and constantly reminded me of the potential this book has to reach millions of women. His presence is needed, not just for this book but every day of my life! He is my earth angel and I thank God for him every single day!

Sulai, my friend of 22 years who I met prior to my husband was the person who led me to Christ. I am thankful she looked past the wounded girl with a chip on her shoulder. She provided space for me to shed masks which revealed the authentic Erica. If I didn't accept her invitation to the church on Cooley Ave., then I would've never met my soulmate. I am forever grateful for her obedience to share the love of Jesus and her courage to look past what was in the flesh and trust the process.

My book coach Rocky Callen was the pilot on helping me transform my wounds, scars, and pain into strength. She provided a sacred space for me to deeply heal and have bigger impact with my message. She helped me see myself as a writer, which was something I lacked confidence in. I am thankful for her support and insight she provided from conception until the birth of my message to the world to inspire many lives.

In addition, I would like to acknowledge my tribe who have been following me through it all from the time I started Fit4life mission as a Personal Trainer and Weight loss coach. I know I have transitioned to a different path and everyone has been very supportive of my aspirations and accomplishments.

Lastly, I would like to acknowledge you my friend, I want you to take these stories and messages to heart and know that I am her to support you along the way. I commend you on taking a step into the direction of creating the life which God has called you to partake in and I thank you for entrusting me to be a part of your story.

ABOUT THE AUTHOR

Erica Stepteau is a dynamic and tenacious motivational speaker, who has empowered women to rise up and claim their unstoppable power regardless of their obstacles or past experiences. One of the tenacious paths she is known for is maintaining joy and hope in a **13-year journey towards fertility** journey which she has experienced 4 natural miscarriages, failed IVF, failed IUI, countless medicated cycles and a recent diagnosis of Adenomyosis. Regardless of the tragedies she keeps a bright smile on her face and trust that God has a major plan for her life. Her journey has inspired many women to keep hope alive even when their situation looks "impossible "or not clear.

Another example of Erica's tenacity started in January 2009; she slipped on a sheet of black ice and broke almost every bone in her left ankle. The injury, which required 1 plate and 6 screws, incapacitated her for 5months. A visit with an Orthopedic Surgeon pushed her to change her life around. He said, "You'll never do any strenuous activities again". She decided to prove him wrong and was able to tell doctor at her 2-year check-up that she **ran a half marathon in two hours and thirty-three minutes! In addition, she returned to appointment 45lbs lighter. She continued on her weight loss journey by losing 65lbs and competing in TWO fitness bikini fitness competitions.**

Erica's coaching and motivational journey began in 2011 via multiple social media platforms; she used her story as the fuel to help women achieve their health & wellness goals by teaching some of the same principles she adapted on her journey. After several years of coaching women to get into the driver's seat of their wellness, she transitioned her focus on helping women optimize their lives in many other compartments such as self-love, confidence, passion/purpose, and abundant thinking all through insightful mindset and empowerment coaching in her virtual practice. One of her most profound messages she created is titled, **"Cultivate the Queen in You"** – **Stop living as a Pawn …Start living as a Queen.**

Erica is the published author of *Unstoppable Tenacity*: A Memoir and Self-help Guide to Empower Women to Rise up and Claim their Unstoppable Power. This book reveals all of the traumatic childhood & adult experiences which has shaped her into the person she is today and how her path was designed by God to boldly share the message to **never give up and never settle for less**. In addition, Erica is currently enrolled in a Public Health Doctoral program to further her education with an expected graduation date of 2018. She lives, plays and works in Cleveland, Ohio and has **huge intentions on sharing her message "Unstoppable Tenacity" around the world!**

Erica Stepteau, MPH
Tenacity & Empowerment Coach
Motivational Speaker
Author

NOTES & RECOMMENDED READINGS

SECTION 1: MAKE SPACE FOR THE VISION

Baylor Barbee, *Life is a Game of Chess,*
www.baylorbarbee.com
Richard Steps Strengths Test
http://richardstep.com/richardstepstrengthsweaknessesaptitude-test/free-aptitude-test-findyour-strengths-weaknesses-online-version/
Myer Briggs
Strengths Based Leadership
Keirsy Temperament Personality Profile
Daring Greatly- Dr. Brene Brown
Water Theory- Dr. Masaru Emoto
Angel Numbers 101-Doreen Virtue
Gary Chapman, *The Five Love Languages*

SECTION 2: CREATE THE VISION

Alison Gopnik, author of The Philosophical Baby: What Children's Minds Tell Us about Truth, Love, and the Meaning of Life
Gabrielle Bernstein, Miracles Now
Steve Harvey, *Act like a Success Think like a Success* Lisa Nichols, *Abundance Now*
Rhonda Byrne, *The Secret*
John Assaraf, *Train your Brain: The Neuroscience of Financial Success*
Oprah's virtual vision board on www.dreamitalive.com
Jim Loehr and Tony Schwartz, *The Power of Full Engagement*

SECTION 3: OVERCOME THE OBSTACLES
Lis Nichols, *No Matter What*
Karen Salmansohn, *The Bounce Back Book*
J. Donald Walters, *Money Magnetism – How to Attract what you Need When you Need it*
John Maxwell, *Failing Forward*
Marie Kundo, *The Art of Tyding Up*
Rev. Linda Martella-Whitsett, *The Mighty Caterpillar*
Type Talk at Work-How the 16 Personality Types Determine Your Success on the Job
Dave Ramsey, *Financial Peace University,* Suze Orman
Robert Kiyosaki,*Rich Dad, Poor Dad*

SECTION 4: ONWARD + BEYOND
William Bridges, *Managing Transitions*
Corboy, co-author, *The Mindfulness Workbook for OCD*
Eckhart Tolle, *The Power of Now*
Peter Drucker, *The of Management* Chris Guillbew, *The Art of Non-conformity* Sen. *Calm Down Mind*: http://www.calmdownmind.com/channelyoursexualenergy/
Mateo Sol: *Transforming Sexual Energy into Spiritual Energy* https://lonerwolf.com/transforming-sexual-energy/